ENGLUND

Trønderlag of America
Centennial
1908-2008

Norskbok
Norskbok Press
Cary, IL

Trønderlag of America Centennial 1908-2008

Library of Congress Control Number: 2008905218

ISBN 0976891131

Editor: Linda K. Schwartz

Cover Design: Liz Schwartz

Production: Norskbok Press

Copyright © 2008 by Trønderlag of America. Manufactured in the United States of America. All rights reserved. No part of this book may be reproduced in any form or by any electronic or mechanical means including information storage and retrieval systems without permission in writing from the publisher, except by a reviewer, who may quote brief passages in a review.

Norskbok Press
PO Box 14
Cary, IL 60013-0014
publisher@norskbok.com

Table of Contents

Dedication: "Greetings to Trønderlag" (O.S.Sneve) . . . iv
From the President vi
Centennial Program 1
2007-2008 Officers & Board of Directors 4
    Norwegian National Anthem: "Ja, Vi Elsker Dette Landet" . 5
    "Nidelven" 6
    Greetings & Congratulations 7
The Beginning: Trønderlag of America 11
    New Banner: Trønders are a Pilgrim People 24
    Local Trønderlaget 25
    2007 Trønderlag Group Photo 26
    "Sons and Daughters" by D. G. Ristad 27
    Historical List of Stevne Sites & Officers 31
    What is a Bygdelag? 43
The Land of a Thousand Lakes 45
    Otter Tail County, Minnesota in 1908 56
Nord- & Sør-Trøndelag Maps 57
Current Trøndelag Kommuner 59
List of Charter Members 1908-1909 61
Charter Members Brief Biographies 65
Living Charter Member Descendants 113
The Final Word: Mange Takk! 136

Greetings to Trønderlag!

by Charter Member O.S. Sneve - 17 Septembre 1908

Translated from Norwegian by Trønder Robert M. Fossum - 10 Mai 2008

They whispered in our ears
That a Trønder is boring and dim-witted
And is only good at driving oxen
But I don't believe that yarn.

Of course he takes things as they come
And doesn't run a race against time
He doesn't expect others to yield by banging on a kettledrum
    or honking the horn
When the way is narrow and steep.

Clearly his blood doesn't boil
Like his brothers from the South
But with hands and head and courage held high
It is good, special what a Trønder does.

Clearly he often ponders and broods
While others act.
But while the southerners stumble
Ola stands on his two legs-both straight and strong as the
    spokes of a wheel.

When one asks where the Trønders are
While the others gather in their lags
It can now be said:
"Here we come, Dear. We have gathered today."

Yes, here we come, young and old.
And at the side of the folk from Valdres and Gudbrandsdalen
We are many, large and strong, and
As a rule we can take care of ourselves.

TRØNDERLAG CENTENNIAL CELEBRATION

All the way from Dovre to Nordland
From Kjølen[1] on the east to Smøla[2] in the west
Trønders grow large and strong
Trønders from farmers to priests[3]

So welcome to the camp boys and girls.
There is hope for an unusually good troop
Now that the Trønders have finally determined
To move their valuable bodies.

Fra Ole S. Sneve's bok "Samlede Sange og Digte"
Utgitt på forfatterens forlag, Silvana, Washington, 1912.

The poem was written to commemorate the founding of
Trønderlaget of America on 17 September 1908.

---

1 *on the Swedish border*
2 *on the west coast of Trøndelag*
3 *indicating a sense of social ladder climbing*

From the President . . .

Centennial Celebration!
Join us August 9, 2008
Fergus Falls, Minnesota
www.tronderlag.org/centennial.htm

August 9, 2008

Dear Trønderlag Members:

Let me extend my congratulations to each of you for helping Trønderlag of America reach the 100th Anniversary of its founding. Without your active supportive, there would be no Trønderlag organization.

As you read through the lag history section of this book, you will learn that maintaining the organization has not always been an easy task. For several years, Trønderlag was disbanded for lack of participation. The individuals to whom we should be most grateful are those who worked to re-establish Trønderlag in 1980-81. This became a turning point in Trønderlag's history.

As our society has grown and evolved, our organization has also changed. It is no longer composed of mostly first or second generation Norwegian-Americans. Many of us are removed from our Norwegian and Trønder heritage by three, four or even five generations. Today's world is a much different place than when our emigrant ancestors left Trøndelag and arrived in America. There are many more opportunities and distractions for each of us.

Please don't let another generation pass without encouraging your children and grandchildren to learn more about their Norwegian family and heritage. I challenge each of you to preserve what you know about your Norwegian legacy. Put it into print. Allow it to prevail for future generations.

To those in attendance at the Centennial Celebration today, my wishes are for each of you to enjoy the program and learn a little more about your Norwegian heritage. Thank you for your continued support of Trønderlag of America!

Sincerely,

Linda

Linda K. Schwartz
President, Trønderlag of America

Program

Centennial Program

Bigwood Event Center – Fergus Falls, Minnesota
Saturday, August 9, 2008

9:00-11:00 am   Trønderlag Centennial Genealogy Lab open

9:30-11:30 am & 12:30-6:00 pm
    Trønder Sales Table open in lobby
    (books, Centennial pins, tote bags, etc.)

12:30-1:30 pm   Centennial Registration

12:30-6:00 pm   History and Genealogy Displays in lobby

1:30 pm   Opening Ceremony (Emcee: Gary Flatgard)
    Kempfer-Adams Room
    National Anthems (accomp. Johanna Hocker)
    Welcome & Introductions
    Greetings from VIPs

2:00 pm   Presentation: What is Trønderlag (Elaine Hasleton)
    Norwegian & Trønder music by Arna Rennan
    Coffee Break

3:30 pm   Presentation: Salute to the Founders (Elaine Hasleton, Robert Fossum, Linda Schwartz)
    Greetings from Descendants
    Short Group Sing (led by Johanna Hocker)

5:00 pm   Close of afternoon program

6:30 pm   Centennial Group Photo by Gregg Vieregge of Images Forever, Alexandria, MN.
    Order an 8 x 10 print of the photo for $12
    Wear your bunad if you have one

TRØNDERLAG CENTENNIAL CELEBRATION

7:00 pm   Centennial Banquet (Emcee: Gary Flatgard)
                  Recognition of Descendants

8:15-10:00 pm   Trønder Sales Table open

                  Drawing for Door Prizes begins (Pat Peterson)

8:30 pm   Trønder Dance and Music by Charter Descendant
                  Mikkel Thompson accompanied by Anders Persson

9:30 pm   Music for Dancing and Listening by the Hjorten
                  Husorkester from Trondheim, Norway

11:30 pm   Close of the Centennial Program

Arna Rennan

Arna's parents emigrated from Norway in the 1950s, imparting to her their world of music and culture. She later studied art and lived in Norway 15 years. Her repertoire includes a wide range, from ballads from the Middle Ages, stev (four-lined poems sung in free rhythm), work songs, immigrant songs, and much more. Her songs reflect history, folklore, religious beliefs, universal themes, and comical frankness. In addition to singing, she plays the guitar, accordion, seljefloyte (overtone flute) and langeleik. She has also recorded a CD titled "Nordic Shores."

Mikkel Thompson

Mikkel Thompson of Sweden and Minnesota has been dancing all his life. He learned gammaldans (waltz, reinlender) through family tradition growing up in northern Minnesota. He started dancing other types of folk

Program

dances in the early 1980's, including springar and gangar in 1985. Mikkel was the Artistic Director of the Nordahl Grieg Leikarring and Barneleikarring in San Jose, California from 1985 to 2002. Mikkel has traveled to Norway many times to study dance and has learned from Karin Brennesvik and Olav Sem, among many others. In the photo at right, Mikkel performs with frequent dance partner Ruth Sylte of Northfield, MN.

Hjorten Husorkester

Hjorten Husorkester is a group of musicians living in Trondheim, the capitol of Trøndelag. There are four members playing in the group, Bjarte Oye (tuba), Roy Morkemo (guitar and accordion), Jan Krogstad (harmonica and accordion) and Berit Boysen (accordion). The group plays folk music and ballads, mostly from Trøndelag, but also from other areas and countries.

Hjorten Husorkester plays regularly at Hjorten Omsorgssenter, a nursing home for elderly people in Trondheim. The oldest people living there are nearly 100 years. The music is popular and inspires people to dance and sing.

The name Hjorten has its own story. From 1859-1961 a remarkable house called Hjorten – Trondhjems tivoli, was then situated at the place where Hjorten Omsorgssenter is now located. Hjorten was a popular place, with cabarets, music, dance, and restaurants. In other words, a good tradition to be followed.

2007-2008 Officers & Board of Directors

President: Linda K. Schwartz - Cary, IL
Vice President: Elaine H. Hasleton - Centerville, UT
Secretary: Nancy Hawkinson - Hudson, WI
Treasurer: Robert Fossum - Champaign, IL
Board: Barry Dahl (Genealogist) - Rochester, MN
Oddgeir Fossli - Inderøy, Norway
Doris Moffett - Moose Lake, MN
Robert Moffett - Moose Lake, MN
Patricia Peterson - Cook, MN & Tucson, AZ
Jon Satrum - Downers Grove, IL

Centennial Committee: Elaine Hasleton, Chair; John Andrisen, Mary Benson, Barry Dahl, Gary Flatgard, Marcia Hansen, Gene Hanson (deceased), Nancy Hawkinson, Bob & Doris Moffett, Patricia Peterson, Maxine Sandvig, Jon Satrum, Linda Schwartz, Gerald Ziesemer

Charter Member Researchers: John Andrisen, Margit Bakke, Mary Benson, Teri Bevan, Barry Dahl, Julia Dixon, Joanne Englund, Carol Greseth, Elaine Hasleton, Nancy Hawkinson, Jo Anne Sadler, Maxine Sandvig, Linda Schwartz, Darlene Stadsvold

Left: Several Board members at Stevne 2007, from left: Nancy Hawkinson, Gene Hanson, Elaine Hasleton, Jon Satrum, Linda Schwartz, and Robert Fossum. Not pictured: Barry Dahl, Oddgeir Fossli, Bob & Doris Moffett, Pat Peterson

Program

Ja, vi elsker dette landet
(Yes, We Love this Land of Ours)

Ja, vi elsker dette landet,

som det stiger frem,

furet, værbitt over vannet,

med de tusen hjem.

Elsker, elsker det og tenker

på vår far og mor

og den saganatt som senker

drømme på vår jord,

og den saganatt som senker

drømme på vår jord.

The lyrics were written by Bjørnstjerne Bjørnson between 1859 and 1868, and the melody was written by his cousin Rikard Nordraak in 1864.

"NIDELVEN STILLE OG VAKKER DU ER..."

Trondheim is the 3rd largest town in Norway, with about 160,000 inhabitants. The town celebrated 1000 years in 1997. Trondheim is a beautiful town in the middle of Norway, where the river Nidelven passes through the center of town.

The following song about Nidelven is known way outside the borders of Trondheim. Den gamle bybro – the old bridge – is mentioned in the song as the gate of happiness. This song is popular in Trondheim as well as in many other countries.

TRØNDERLAG CENTENNIAL CELEBRATION

Nidelven

Langt i det fjerne bak fjellene blå
Ligger et sted jeg har kjær.
Dit mine tanker og drømmer vil gå,
Alltid du er meg så nær.

Nidelven stille og vakker du er
Her hvor jeg går og drømmer.
Drømmer om deg som jeg hadde så kjær,
Nu er det bare minner.

Den gamle bybro er lykkens portal
Sammen vi seiler i stjernekorall.
Nidelven, stille og vakker du er
Her hvor jeg går og drømmer.

Tekst: Oscar Hodde; Melodi: Christian Christensen og Kjell Rian

Greetings & Congratulations!

Rådhusgt. 23 B
NO-0158 Oslo, Norway
Tel. +47 23 35 71 70
Fax +47 23 35 71 75
norseman@norseman.no
www.norseman.no

Oslo, April 28, 2008

Linda K. Schwartz, President
Trønderlag of America
7001 Owl Way
Cary, IL 60013, USA

Dear Linda K. Schwartz:

Thank you very much for your kind invitation for us to be represented at the centennial celebration for the Trønderlag of America to be held on August 9. Regretfully, Georg A. Broch is no longer our Secretary General and the Board of Directors is in the process of finding a replacement. However, the Board of Directors and staff members join in sending you our heartiest congratulations on this important milestone in your organization's history and in wishing you a successful celebration!

Like the *bygdelag* in America, Nordmanns-Forbundet (now in its 101st year) has as its purpose the strengthening of ties between emigrated Norwegians and their descendants around the world with Norway. Therefore no other organization in Norway understands better than we do the impact and importance the *bygdelag* movement has had in America—and continues to have—for its members to maintain contact with the rural Norwegian communities from which many of the emigrants and their descendants originated.

We hope you will send us a report, with photographs, on the Centennial celebration so that we can publish this information in our magazine *The Norseman*.

Very sincerely yours,

Harry T. Cleven

Harry T. Cleven, Editor
The Norseman

DIS-Norge
Databehandling i slektsforskning

Date: Mon, 12 May 2008 22:01:39 +0200

From: "Torill Johnsen" <torillj@gmail.com>

To: "Linda Schwartz" <president@tronderlag.org>

Subject: Re: Trønderlag of America Centennial

We would like to extend our greetings to you, members of Trønderlag of America, on the centennial celebration.

We, DIS-Norway central organization and regional branch Trøndelag, are pleased to be able to establish and improve contacts with you. This might give your members as well as our members, better opportunities in the future. Both sides being interested in Norwegian roots and American as well as Norwegian ancestry.

We wish you all the best for the celebration this year and look forward to many opportunities in the future for joint activities.

Med hilsen

Torill Johnsen
President of Genealogy Society of Norway-DIS

Torill Aasegg
President of Genealogy Society of Sør-Trøndelag-DIS

GREETINGS & CONGRATULATIONS!

April 30, 2008

Gratulerer med 100 års jubileum!

   Since the Trønderlag of America was founded, it has experienced historical change but it persevered to reach this year to reflect and be glad with other members and friends. You have made special plans for this centennial year and it is time to celebrate and enjoy your legacy until now--and to leave traditions to benefit all follow in the future.

   Sincere congratulations from the entire Fellesraad board, which represents all of our affiliated sister bygdelag. May your good leadership, family history research and ties with Norway, and your publications continue to inspire and serve your members!

Marilyn Dahlen Somdahl, President
Bygdelagenes Fellesraad
www.fellesraad.com

May 1, 2008
To: Linda K. Schwartz, President
Trønderlag of America

Hey!

My English is not very good, but I try to send you an answer to your invitation. Hope you understand!

I'm the leader of DIS-Nord-Trøndelag and I have received the invitation to your Centennial Celebration at 9th of August. It would be exciting to travel "over there" and take part in your celebration. Many of our members are searching for their ancestors in USA and are interesting in what happens on the other side of the Atlantic Ocean. But I'm sorry to say that I can't answer yes to your invitation at this moment. Today's circumstances of life and the costs tell me that the journey will be difficult to carry out. The situation could perhaps be different later in the summer, but now by May 1, I have to say no.

I'm sure you get a great Celebration, and I and my organization (DIS-Nord-Trøndelag) wish you good luck with the Centennial Celebration, and the best greetings for the next hundred years with genealogy among "American Tronderlags peoples" !

Sincerely,

Per Herstad
Leader DIS-Nord-Trøndelag

The Beginning: Trønderlag of America

In March of 1904 a group of Trønders got together to plan a Trønderlaget stevne, but abandoned the idea because of bickering over what territory in Norway they should include. They were afraid they would cut a poor figure in comparison with the Valders group who organized in 1899. A Trønderlag was hastily created in June of 1907 but received little support and failed.

Before the first real national meeting in 1908, there had been much writing and correspondence in the Norwegian papers, *Scandinavian* and *Decorah Posten*. They had a difficult time finding someone to take the leadership. Faculty members of Trønder background at Park Region College in Fergus Falls, headed by the president Rev. D. G. Ristad, were among the promoters. Prof. Thomas Wollan and Prof. I. Dorrum on their own called an organizational meeting. All Tronders from the eight fylkes were to be included.

The group was organized on 17 September 1908 in Fergus Falls, Minnesota under the name *Trønderlaget of America*. A notice in a Fergus Falls newspaper (shown right) announced the meeting. The primary organizers included Ditlef G. Ristad and S. O. Leirfallom among others.

A report from the *Fergus Falls Daily Journal* on the morning of September 17, 1908 said:

> **TRONDERE ATTENTION!**
>
> On the 17th of this month the Trondere will gather in Norden Hall, Fergus Falls, to effect an organization for the purpose of keeping alive the splendid traditions of old Trondelagen and make arrangements for future meetings, and transact such other business as may come up before the meeting.
>
> Vice-consul and editor of the Decorah Posten Joh's B. Wist will address the meeting, also President Kildahl of St. Olaf College and other prominent and eloquent men of Tronder stock.
>
> In the evening a banquet will be spread, music, singing and bright toasts. Come all, -- come and bring enthusiasm and good cheer.
>
> In behalf of the committee,
>
> D. G. Ristad

The Fergus Falls Free Press, September 9, 1908, p. 5

TRØNDERLAG CENTENNIAL CELEBRATION

A meeting is being held in this city today for the purpose of organizing a Trondelag — that is, an organization of the people of this and adjoining states who came originally from Trondelagan, Norway.

The meeting was called by Rev. S. U. [sic] Leirfall (Sivert O. Leirfallom), of Mohall, N.D. and the suggestion that a reunion of this kind be arranged has met with a hearty response, fully one hundred and fifty people from outside points being in attendance. Johannes Wist, editor of the Decorah Posten, and several other distinguished gentlemen are here and will deliver addresses this afternoon and tonight.

The gathering convened at Norden hall during the forenoon, Rev. S. O. Leirfall presiding, and Prof. Dorrum of this city, acting as secretary. The forenoon session was devoted to enrollment and getting acquainted.

The meeting this afternoon is to take place at the court house, and it is expected that a permanent organization will be formed and arrangements will be made for holding annual reunions.

The visitors will be tendered a banquet at the Park hotel this evening. The affair gives promise of proving a very pleasant and successful gathering from every standpoint."

ABOVE: *The original Otter Tail County Court House where the Tronders met to form the organization on 17 September 1908.*

A further report on the event was found in the *Fergus Falls Daily Journal*, September 18, 1908:

TRONDELAG

A Big Reunion Held in This City and a Permanent Organization is Formed – The Officers

Trønderlag History

*Vice Consul Wist Speaks in the
Afternoon and an Enjoyable Banquet is
Held in the Evening.*

The reunion of the people of Trondelagen, which was held in this city Thursday, was one of the most enjoyable gatherings of the season, and was attended by delegates from North Dakota, Iowa and other states, as well as from all parts of Minnesota.

The forenoon session was held in Norden Hall, as stated Thursday, and the afternoon session at the court house. The address of welcome was delivered by Prof. Ristad and it was planned to have County Attorney Elect Anton Thompson respond on behalf of the visitors, but he was compelled to leave for home and his brother John B. Thompson took his place. The principal address of the afternoon was by Vice Consul J. B. Wist, editor of the Decorah Posten, at Decorah, Iowa and was pleasing, entertaining and appropriate to the occasion.

A permanent organization was formed during the afternoon with the following officers:

President, M. A. Wollan, of Glenwood, Minn.

Vice President, O. O. Hauan, of Mayville, N. D.

Secretary and treasurer, Rev. S. O. Leirfall, of Mohall, N. D.

Directors, Vice Consul J. B. Wist, Decorah, J. N. Kildahl, president of St. Olaf college, Northfield, Prof. K. Gjerseth, of Decorah, Dr. Warlow, of Chicago, and Prof. Ristad of this city.

The time and place for holding the next reunion was left to the executive committee.

Mr. Wollan, the president of the organization, is a well known banker of Glenwood.

The gathering closed with an evening banquet at the Park hotel. The banquet itself was all that could be desired, the bill of fare including a delicious spread of the best of everything appetizing, and B. B. Haugan acted as toastmaster of the evening, toasts being responded to by Mr. Wincher of Brandon, O. O. Hauan, the vice president, Editor Middlefart of the Forum at Fargo, Editor Wist, Dr. Vigen, Theodore Johnson and Prof. Ristad of this city and M.A. Wollan. Prof. Veblen, of Stilllwater, who is president of Valders-Samband, was also present and was admitted as an honorary member. He spoke entertainingly during the evening and as president of a

13

similar organization, which has not been in existence for several years, gave the Trondelag a great deal of valuable information and advice.

The banquet lasted until a late hour, and at its conclusion, a number of the visitors left for their homes on the night trains, others going this morning.

Another report was presented a few days later by the *Fergus Falls Free Press* on September 23, 1908, page 4:

A HOST OF TROENDERE

*Gathered in Fergus Thursday
and organized Troendelag.
Feasting and Oratory*

The Troendere are not noted for their diffidence or modesty, anyway, but now they are prouder and haughtier than ever. And Why?

O, because they had a meeting in Fergus Falls Thursday that puts them right in the front rank. It was in all respects a grand affair and the Troendere have reason to feel proud when they think about it.

There were Troendere present from about seven different states, although Minnesota furnished most of them. They assembled at Norden Hall in the forenoon, but that place got too small, so they adjourned to the court house. Prof. Ristad of the Park Region Lutheran College, who was the prime mover

Northern Pacific Railway Depot in Fergus Falls, Minnesota, early 1900s
Photo from the Otter Tail County Historical Society

Trønderlag History

in bringing about the meeting, gave the address of welcome; and his speech was so good that it made the Troendere proud that he is one of them. Attorney J. B. Thompson of Battle Lake gave the response, and he too did so well that the pride of the Troendere was given another boost. His brother, Anton Thompson, was slated to make the response, but it being felt that a Troender who could gather in votes the way he did in his race for county attorney, must be both magnetic and eloquent as a talker.

Consul J. B. Wist, editor of the Decorah Posten, was the principal speaker in the afternoon, and his address was thoroughly enjoyed.

In the evening a banquet was pulled off at the Park Hotel, with B. B. Haugan as toastmaster. Toasts were given by Prof. Ristad, M. A. Wollan of Glenwood, O. C. Houan of Mayville, N. Dal., Editor Trovaaten of Fargo, Mr. Wincher of Brandon, Theodore Johnson of Fergus Falls, and Prof. Veblen of Stillwater, who is not a Troender, but a Valdris "Gubbe", like Boen.

A permanent organization, or Troendelag, was formed during the afternoon, and M. A. Wollan, the well known Glenwood banker — a relative of Prof. T. C. Wollan — was elected president. O. C. Hauan of Mayville was elected vice president; Rev. Lerfall of Mohall, N. Dak., secretary-treasurer; Consul Wist, Prof. Ristad, Prof. Kildal of Northfield, Prof. Gjerseth of Decorah, Mr. Warlow of Chicago, directors. These will decide when and where to hold the next annual meeting.

The success of the organizational meeting of Trønderlaget in 1908 led to a second stevne, this one in Glenwood, Pope County, Minnesota. A lengthy report on that stevne was provided by the *Glenwood Herald*, Friday, June 25, 1909:

TRONDERS HOLD
ANNUAL STEVNE

Very Successful Meeting Was Held by Members of "Tronderlaget" on Friday and Saturday.

The annual stevne of Tronderlaget which was held at the lakeshore pavilion last Friday and Saturday was successful beyond expectations.

The lag was originally organized last September at Fergus Falls with 120 members. Since then the membership has increased to more than 500 and will continue to grow by the hundreds in time to come.

At last week's meeting Trondere were present from Michigan, Illinois, Iowa, Wisconsin, North and South Dakota and Minnesota. All of these were enthusiastic over the meeting and will take an active part in furthering the purposes of the organization.

The business meeting was held in the pavilion Friday afternoon at half past two o'clock and was called to order by the president, M. A. Wollan of Glenwood. The secretary, Rev. O. S. Leirfall of Mohall, N.Dak, was not present and Prof. I. Dorrum of Fergus Falls was elected secretary pro tem.

An address of welcome was delivered on behalf of the Tronders of Glenwood and of Pope County by the Rev. G. T. Lee. Rev. Sangseth responded on behalf of the visitors in a very happy manner.

The report of the committee which has been selected at the Fergus Falls meeting to prepare a draft for a constitution was read and upon motion considered by the meeting. The constitution was submitted was discussed by sections and was adopted with a few changes. According to the constitution the purpose of the organization is to work for unity among the Trondere of this country, to preserve the traditions of their ancestor Trondere and to support worthy Norwegian undertakings.

The name of the organization is "Tronderlaget of America." The constitution and by-laws adopted provide for necessary offices, for their duties, for important methods of procedure in annual meetings and for other matters essential to such an organization.

A committee on nominations of officers was appointed and consisted of the following gentlemen:

Consul H. Bendeke of Grand Forks, Peter Lein of Fergus Falls, A. O. Heglie of Walcot, D. C. Jordahl of Norway Lake and S. S. Oksness of Doran.

According to the recommendations of the committee the following officers were elected for the ensuing year:

President - M. A. Wollan, Glenwood, Minn.

Vice presidents - Ole M. Olson Five, Fort Dodge, Ia; Rev. D. C. Jordahl, Norway Lake, Minn.; N. Grevstad, Chicago, Ill.; Consul H. Bendeke, Grand Forks, N.D.; Syver S. Oksness, Doran, Minn.; Prof. C. Christianson, Sioux Falls, S. Dak.

Secretary-treasurer - Prof. T. C. Wollan, Fergus Falls, Minn.

TRØNDERLAG HISTORY

Directors for three years – Prof. D. G. Ristad, Fergus Falls, Minn., Consul J. B. Wist, Decorah, Ia.

Directors for two years – Dr. Thomas Warloe, Chicago, Ill.; Hon. O. M. Hauan, Mayville, N. Dak.

Directors for one year – A. C. Floan, St. Paul; L. Hoymeth, Ishpeming, Mich.

T. C. Wollan was called upon to explain his proposed system to secure historical information about Trondere who have settled in this country and to prepare this information.

Mr. Wollan explained that the card system would be used. Printed cards have been and will be distributed. All Trondere will be requested to fill in those cards with the important facts about their lives. These cards will be arranged alphabetically and will be kept by the secretary. In time a book containing the information thus secured will be printed.

Other matters of importance were also brought up for discussion at Friday afternoon's session but were laid over until Saturday when another business session was held.

A board of audit of two members was appointed by the president, consisting of Gunder Dahl of Fergus Falls and Samuel Haugdal of St. Peter.

Friday evening at six o'clock a Norwegian supper was served in the tent under the supervision of Edwin Kaldahl. Rommegrodt, lefse and other courses were in evidence. Tickets for the supper were sold at fifty cents.

The main program was carried out at eight o'clock. The Glenwood band under the direction of Prof. O. K. Onlie played a few selections before the meeting opened.

The following program was rendered:
Vocal solo – Holger Wollan
Song – Ladies Octette
Address – Dr. Thos. Warloe
Ja vi Elsker – Laget
Reading from Suutikjagta – Mrs. Thos. Warloe
Address for squaw men – Rev. G. T. Lee
Ten minute speeches – P. O. Stromme, Prof. I. Dorrum, Rev. D. C. Jordahl.

At the business session on Saturday morning the proposed commemoration gift to Norway in 1914 was discussed. Inasmuch as a large part of the large gift which Norwegians in this country will give to the mother country at the centennial celebration in 1914 is intended for the cathedral at Trondhjem the lag passed unanimously a resolution pledging its support to the gift movement.

Prof. Ristad called attention to the efforts of two men in Norway to preserve Tronder traditions and history. One of those, Caud. Braseth, has made a special study of traditions and customs and has prepared a manuscript for publication in the Selbu dialect. The other, Henrick Mathison, has written a history of Trondjem's cathedral in several volumes. Both of these man have spent considerable time and money in preparing their works. They are also poor and need assistance and encouragement. The lag passed resolutions recommending that the members subscribe for the two books and encourage the authors in their efforts.

The matter of an official organ for the society was also discussed but was on motion laid over until the next annual meeting.

The following is a list of the names of Tronder who were present at the banquet:

Minnesota — Mr. and Mrs. M. E. Anderson, Barrett; Frances Anderson, Barrett; Mr. and Mrs. A. M. Anderson, Barrett; Mrs. Julia Kalheim, Farmington; J. W. Rosholt, Pelican Rapids; M. Saxtnan, Brandon ; Ole Nygaard, Fergus Falls; Mrs. O. P. Olson, Madison; Mr. and Mrs. Ingolf Peterson, Morris; Miss Ingeborg Kasseth, Pelican Rapids; Mr. and Mrs. Ole J. Kasseth, Pelican Rapids; Ingolf Velde, Brainard; Christian Fiskness, Alexandria; L. Sorass, Hayfield; John Nornborg, Evansville; Ole Nelson, Hancock; Sam Haugdahl, St.Peter; O. P. Borstad, Madison; Bee Bolland, Marietta; G. J. Lund, Madison; Peder Benson, Kensington; Mr. and Mrs. G. T. Winkjer, Garfield; J. Thompson, Brandon; Mr. and Mrs. B. O. Solberg, Brandon; Mr. and Mrs. J. R. Skogrand, Watson; Mrs. Paul Foslin, Garfield; Mr. and Mrs. J. P. Haave, Fergus Falls; Mr. and Mrs. M. O. Ulstad, Madison; R. Benson, Kensington; Mrs. W. R. Hurd, Madison; D. C. Jordahl, Norway Lake; Mr. and Mrs. A. Sumstad, Ashby; A. Gjerset, Fergus Falls; Henry Anderson, Watson; Anna Norman, Ashby; Mr. and Mrs. B. O. Koefod, Ashby; R. T. Morieth, Appleton; Johannes P. Schei, Dalton; Ole E. Lien, Madison; Albert Forbord, Benson; Casper Forbord, Clontarf; A. A. Henningsgaard, Marietta; C. Mindrum, Hanley; J. J. Lofthaug, Sherburne Co.; N. Hanson, Dalton; T. C. Wollan, Fergus Falls; Jonas Hallan, Fergus Falls; I. R. Rosholt, Pelican Rapids; Carl Rosholt, Fergus Falls; O. Johnson, Fergus Falls; Martin Aalberg, Henning; Mr. and Mrs. A. H. Slotave, Ashby; H. Slotane, Barrett; P. Langseth, Princeton; Mrs. Dorah Wig, Brooten; Ole O. Wig, Brooten; E.

P. Alstad, Milan; Ing. Odun, Montevideo; H. J. Moe, Rushford; Mrs. Ellen Skogrand, Montevideo; Karen Odegaard, Montevideo; T. T. Odegaard, Montevideo; Mrs. B. Dahl, Dalton; Theo E. Stras, Rothsay; Iver Skistad, Elizabeth; O. J. Oblaug, Madison; A. Ingebretson, Brandon; Ed. Thorson, Spring Grove; D. G. Ristad, Fergus Falls; G. L. Islaud, Elbow Lake; J. O. Strand, Elbow Lake; J. Johnson, Madison; A. P. Strinden, Pelican Rapids; R. Ristad, Fergus Falls; Mrs. P. Kelstup, Hoffman; Mrs. K. K. Sletten, Hoffman; G. O. Dahl, Fergus Falls; C. Aasnes, Fergus Falls; H. Snee, Garfield; Otto Tollefson, Clontarf; H. J. Eggen, Garfield; L. P. Floan, Clontarf; D. C. Stokke, Kenyon; O. J. Dahl, Newfolden; Mr. and Mrs. A. M. Skrove, Dalton; Mrs. Ole P. Flaten, Granite Falls; A. J. Evenson, Osakis; M. Hagen, Morris; J. J. Angen, Garfield; Peter Lein, Fergus Falls; Mrs. L. Hustad, Kensington; Mr. and Mrs. Syver Oksnes, Doran; Clara Oksnes, Doran; P. R. Sletten, Pennock; Mrs. K. Foslin, Garfield.

Pope County — Mr. and Mrs. Ben Evjen, Mr. and Mrs. A. Ranum, Mr. and Mrs. L. Heggestad, Mr. and Mrs. A. Stoen, Mr. and Mrs. B. M. Tessem, Mr. and Mrs. L. C. Gorder, Mr. and Mrs. Peter Berg, Mr. and Mrs. M. P. Eidberg, Rev. and Mrs. Forda, Mr. and Mrs. H. L. Gorder, Mr. and Mrs. J. C. Gorder, Mr. and Mrs. H. Rosby, Mr. and Mrs. Conrad Siverson, A. Bardal, Mrs. C. C. Gorder, Arne Stoen, G. O. Forde, Mr. and Mrs. J. C. Gorder, Mr. and Mrs. A. Holte, C. Brors, Carl Lingen, Mrs. J. B. Ness, Annie Ness, Ole L. Johnson, M. N. Ellie, Iver Aal, Mrs. B. Holte, A. P. Norby, Mrs. O. Horjem, H. O. Kirkevold, L. A. Giskaas, M. Deraas, Einar Johnson, M. Opdal, Ole Overstad, Mrs. P. Benson, B. C. Wollan, Louise Finstad, Bertine Tharaldson, Mrs. R. Wollan, Mrs. P. Kaldahl, Mr. and Mrs. J. T. Rotto, Martin, Isak and Ruth Rotto, J. Finstad, M. Aasum, A. J. Kippe, M. Engebretson, Mrs. C. Kittleson, Netta Wollan, Elmer Onseth, Mr. and Mrs. L. K. Omseth, O. E. Ormseth, B. E. Ormseth, Mr. and Mrs. Jno. Gunvaldson, Mr. and Mrs. O. P. Hjermstad, Mrs. J. Hafstad, C. E. Brown, Mrs. Mattie Tande, Julia Tharaldson, C. S. Lee, Mr. and Mrs. B. Troen, Sven Rosten, S. Ramstad, Ida Dyrstad, Mr. and Mrs. John Dyrstad, Mable Dyrstad, P. Troen, Marie Troen, Mr. and Mrs. K. Torguson, A. Plateon, and a large number of people from the village.

North Dakota — Edward Berg, Landa; G. R. Estrem, Reeder; Mrs. Andrew Haugen, Landa; Ole N. Ydstie, Hillsboro; O. C. Hauan, Mayville; Mrs. Olaf Crogan, Kramer; A. C. Heglie, Walcott; Mr. and Mrs. John N. Horsager, Litchville; Consul H. Bendeke, Grand Forks; Gina N. Horsager,

Litchville; Mrs. O. M. Ramstad, Landa; Magda Ramstad, Landa; John Hammer, Kathryn; Andrew Peterson, Eaglevale; P. O. Nesseth, Galenburg; Ellef Tolstad, Valley City; O. Selbo, Valley City; Barbara Wollan, Landa; Helmer Frederickson, Kindred; Johan Frederickson, Kindred; George Larson, Ashley.

South Dakota — Oluf Beistad, Effington; Mada Raaen, Effington; Engebrigt Johnson, Sisseton; C. Lee, Colman; Bella Landrud, Pennville; Anton Hegg, Garreton; E. Hammer, Sherman; Ole Sagness, Sherman; Borghild Hatling, Effington; P. O. Nold, Colman; Oluf Moe, Galesburg; C. Christiunson, Sioux Falls; Sovering Pederson, Effington.

Michigan — Lars Hoyseth, Ishpeming.

Illinois — Dr. Thomas Warloe, Chicago; Signa Warloe, Chicago.

Wisconsin — Inga Neerlund, Amery; Peer Stromme, Madison; L. J. Oyaas, Superior.

Iowa — Ove C. Johnson, Decorah; Mr. and Mrs. A. M. Rovelstad, Decorah; E. G. Mellem, Northwood; B. J. Geving, Decorah.

Norway — Mrs. Dick Waaler, Kristiania; Fasto Swenson, Trondhjem.

The majority of those attending early stevner (annual meetings) were first generation immigrants in America. Attending a stevne afforded an opportunity to renew acquaintances with those from their home area of Norway. In its early years, the main purpose of the stevne was social. It provided an opportunity for early immigrants to get together to speak the Norwegian language (and Trondersk dialect) and share their stories from the homeland as well as their stories and experiences in America.

In 1908 there were 120 charter members, most of whom were born in Norway. More than 400 joined before the next stevne in 1909. Membership grew to 2,556 by 1925. As a comparison, in 2008 Trønderlag has slightly more than 500 members with attendance of Trønders at the annual stevne at about 85-90.

In its formative years the Trønderlaget published a number of yearbooks. Its members were early members of Nordmans-Forbundet. They also helped organize the Bygdelagenes Fellesraad. Money to help build a Kors Altar (choir altar) was donated to

Trønderlag History

Trondheims Domkirke and they also presented an expensive model of Nidaros Kirke to the Norwegian-American Museum at Decorah.

The Trønderlaget organization thrived through the 1920s and 1930s, but was discontinued during WWII. It resumed again in 1946 with a stevne in Appleton, MN. Henry Nycklemoe was the president then. In 1966, due to sparse attendance at the stevne, the Trønderlaget stevne was discontinued.

In 1980, an organizational meeting was held for the purpose of re-organizing the lag. The group consisted of: Agnes Boraas, Floyd and Selma Boraas, Ivin and Anna Kleven, Lowell and Bernice Oellien, Rudy and Bernice Prestholdt, Bevin and Arlene Skjei, Mildred Skurdahl, Ellsworth and Sylvia Smogard, Orvin and Josephine Larson, Selma Tordtenson and Berdeen and Mable Vaala. The re-organized Trønderlag held a stevne June 19-21, 1981 in Appleton, MN and were surprised when almost 400 people attended the banquet. A new banner, pictured here, was created at that time.

Stevner since 1981 have been held in various communities in Minnesota, South Dakota, North Dakota, Iowa and Wisconsin.

In 1999 the lag was renamed "Trønderlag of America" and a new set of by-laws were ratified by members at the business meeting.

In 2001 Trønderlag of America joined together with one other Norwegian-American organization, the Gudbrandsdalslaget, to hold a joint stevne in Starbuck, MN. In 2003, the annual stevne became the "Tre Lag Stevne" with three lags now involved in the planning

21

and participation: Trønderlag, Gudbrandsdalslag, and Nord-Hedmark og Hedemarken lag. It has also grown to a full three-day event. Since then the Tre Lag Stevne has been held in Sioux Falls, SD; Rochester, MN; Fargo, ND; Eau Claire, WI; Onalaska/La Crosse, WI; and this year in Fergus Falls, MN. The Tre Lag Stevne format has been an overwhelming success. Each summer from 200-240 people have attended the Tre Lag Stevne.

In 2002 a new Trønderlag membership pin shown here was created by Herb Mikkelson of Sioux Falls. In November 2002, a web site was established for Trønderlag by Linda Schwartz. This site continues today to provide news of the organization, forms for membership and stevne, and genealogy resources at: www.tronderlag.org

At stevne in August 2005, Trønderlag released a new Aarbok - the first to be published in many years. *Aarbok 2005*, edited by Linda Schwartz, consisted of 424 pages in English which included organization history as well as 126 Trønder immigrant biographies and photos. Earlier aarboker were in Norwegian. The book cover and inside design were created by graphic designer Liz Schwartz.

On August 16, 2005, Trønderlag was Incorporated in the state of Minnesota - the first step in becoming an official non-profit organization. Trønderlag is required to renew this Certificate of Incorporation each year.

On September 8, 2005, 35 lag members departed for Trondheim, Norway as part of the heritage tour organized by Trønderlag. The goal

of the trip was to provide historical background for members as they researched as well as to assist them in locating their family farms and meet their Trønder relatives. All were successful in that endeavor!

By early 2006 planning was well underway for the Centennial. Goals and objectives for the event and a plan for fund-raising were developed, and the Centennial Committee determined that we should try to locate descendants of the original 120 Charter Members of the organization.

A new Constitution and Bylaws were adopted by the membership at the annual meeting in Eau Claire, WI in August 2006. Changes were made to the earlier Bylaws in order to comply with IRS requirements for non-profit status. The organization received 501(c)(3) non-profit status from the IRS in 2007. The 384-page *Aarbok 2006 - Yearbook of the Trønderlag of America* was released at the stevne. *Aarbok 2006* provide firsthand accounts of the immigrant experience in the letters home to Norway and the biographies of more than 80 Trønder immigrant families.

In preparation for the Centennial celebration in 2008 a new Centennial pin was designed using the Centennial logo as its basis. Another aarbok (yearbook) will be published following the Centennial in 2008. The book will include photos and story from the stevne as well as detailed biographies of all Charter Members and many other Trønder immigrants.

In addition, a new banner has been created in 2008 and will be unveiled at the Centennial. The following provides an explanation of the banner design.

23

Trønders are a Pilgrim People - The Message of the New Banner

By Gary Flatgard

Pilgrims are a people who travel. Often they are on their way to sacred places for holy purposes. But that doesn't have to be the way it is all the time for pilgrims. It isn't the way it is for pilgrim Trønders.

Trønders travel, for sure, but it's not usually to sacred places for holy purposes. First, Trønders traveled from Norway to the New Land across the Atlantic to North America as emigrants in the 1800s and early 1900s. They were poor in Norway. There wasn't enough food, land or work for them there, so they moved away. Then Trønders, like you and me, as descendants of the original pilgrims, travel to Norway, the Old Country, for visits with the folks and places there. And Trønders in Norway, also as descendants of the original emigrants, travel to the New Land to visit the folks there, many of whom are their relatives. Yes, Trønders are a pilgrim people, traveling far and wide, east and west across the great divide of the Atlantic Ocean.

The central image on the new Trønderlag of America banner is the pilgrims' marker found in Norway. It's found along the pilgrims' path from Oslo to Trondheim guiding them on their pilgrimages to the Nidaros Cathedral, the burial place of St. Olaf (King Haraldson killed at the battle of Stiklestad in Trøndelag in 1030 A.D.). This marker, in the shape of a cross, was a sign directing the pilgrims to a sacred place for holy purposes.

The image of the pilgrims' marker on the Trønderlag's new banner recalls for us the holy purposes for which the pilgrims went to Nidaros, a very special place. It also reminds us that Trønders are a pilgrim people, journeying a long way to special places here and there, traveling to meet and visit special people here and there. Yes, we Trønders are a pilgrim people!

Local Trønderlaget

Below is a list of the 15 local lags that were organized at one time in addition to the National Trønderlaget:

- Chicago Trønderlag; organized in Chicago in 1924
- Chippewa Valley Trønderlag; organized at Eau Claire, Wis in 1920
- Duluth Trønderlag; organized in Duluth in 1920
- Trønderlag in Everett, WA; organized in Everett in 1955
- Grand Forks Trønderlag; organized in Grand Forks, ND in 1917
- Brulle Trønderlag; organized at Emmett, SD in 1936
- Lake Hendricks Trønderlag; organized at Lake Hendricks in 1930
- Minneapolis Trønderlag; organized at Minneapolis in 1913
- Trønderlag Nidaros; organized at Tacoma, WA in 1927
- The Northwest Trønderlag; organized at Minot, ND in 1929
- Park Region Trønderlag; organized at Ashby, MN in 1926
- Pope County Trønderlag; organized at Starbuck, MN in 1921
- Sioux Valley Trønderlag; organized at Baltic, SD in 1922
- Thief River Falls Trønderlag; organized at Thief River Falls in 1926
- Trønderlaget Tordenskjold; organized in Seattle, WA before 1925

Of these local Trønderlaget, only Trønderlaget in Everett, Washington is still an active organization in 2008.

TRØNDERLAG CENTENNIAL CELEBRATION

2007 Trønderlag of America Group Photo from Stevne at Onalaska, Wisconsin

From left, those who appeared for the photo before the banquet:

Row 1 (front): Linda Schwartz, Sue Dahl, Elaine Hasleton, Lois McCormick, Sharon Engelhardt, Meredith Berg, Carolyn J. Storlie, Johanna Hocker, Kathy Pedersen, Alice M. Brask, Aileen Torrence, Ruthie Herdahl, JoAnne Schroeder, Isabelle Volden, Ann Flisrand, Jo Anne Sadler

Row 2: Ruth Williamson, Barry M. Dahl, Ann Smith, Mike Miller, Ronald Anderson, Barbara Anderson, Marlys Thorsgaard, Yvette Storsved, Kristin McCrea, Deb Nelson Gourley, Margit Bakke, Delores Cleveland, Glenyta Hanson, Gene Hanson, Pete Volden, Richard Flisrand, Marcia Hansen

Row 3: David Williamson, Les Berg, Roger Hanson, Pat Peterson, Trudy DeKeuster, Lyle Elverud, Elsie Elverud, Arlen Thorsgaard, Irving Storsved, Anna Lattu, Nancy Todd, Louise Lang, Robin Fossum, Lanny Sangster, Carolyn Satrum, Jon Satrum, Joanne Johnson

Row 4: Howard Hansen, Rohl Peterson, Joanne Englund, Karen Christensen, Mary Benson, Jim Hocker, Gordon Spidahl, Adele Spidahl, Doris Moffett, Bob Moffett, C. Marvin Lang, Robert Fossum, Wayne Sangster, Lawrence Thompson, Terri Bevan, Harley Johnson

TRØNDERLAG HISTORY

Sons and Daughters*

By D. G. Ristad

The following verses were written for the Trønderlag year book a year or two ago (1932-33). Because of the nature of the message I bring here, I make bold to repeat it in the hope that its appearance may reach those among our American born Trønders who may not have seen it at its first publication:

*By valiant fathers' farflung quest
Your fine estate is won;
And faithful mothers did the rest
To help you carry on.
Their sacrifice, their love and toil
Have made your homestead hallowed soil.*

*The sons that stand where fathers stood
To guard their heritage,
And make it grow, as grow it should,
In worth from age to age –
Our pledge they are and surety
Of all we ever hope to be.*

Professor Ditlef G. Ristad (1863-1938)

*The daughters fair who humbly take
Their sainted mothers' place
To better build and nobler make
The future of our race,
Are greater boon to home and state
Than you and I can calculate.*

*The ardent Youth and tranquil Age,
Wherever they may be,
Together must attempt to gage
Our common destiny:*

* Written on the 25th anniversary of the founding of Trønderlag of America. It was written in English so that future generations would be able to read it. Reprinted from the *1934 Trønderlagets Aarbok*

27

The Old must give to Youth a hold,
And Youth take council from the Old.

The folk today who love the clan,
As in the days of yore,
Are counting on each maid and man
To keep the sacred lore,
And make the ancient epic toll
Its call through ev'ry honest soul.

The passing generations hope to have their best qualities enlarged in the succeeding generations, and to have the children and childrens' children spared from the faults, weakness and mistakes of the parents and their forbearers. They want to love themselves in the lovableness of their own descendants, to live fuller and richer and finer in their children than they were able or permitted to live, and to have fostered in the future the ideals they carried in their souls but could not realize. In this noble aspiration there lies a challenge to Sons and Daughters. It is this challenge we of the first generation of American pioneers from Trøndelagen would pass on to American born Trønders to accept and meet.

In the "Trønderlag of America" we of the immigrant generation have endeavored to foster certain traditions and make effective certain qualities of mind, heart and character that were our heritage from our native Trøndelagen. During the quarter century of our existence as a "lag" we have tried to emphasize those qualities in the Norwegian racial group that are colored by and reflected through our Trønder temperament. The influence of American viewpoints, aims and ideals created a new atmosphere about us but it did not radically change us. The American born generation, on the other hand, imbibed the very life of America; the immediate environment into which they were ushered, determined to a large extent, not only their language, but their view of life; they were molded by American thought in the schools they attended, the books they read and the associates they had. The tendency in the Norwegian character "at føre kraft til andre (to inbue others with their own powers)" made the process of Americanization rather easy, and doubtless a little too hurried.

While this fact cannot be denied, it is still true that those elements in the Norwegian and Trønder personality which have been built up relentlessly and silently during hundreds of years of native influences, sheltered and molded into type in the valleys and along the fjords of Norway, are too fundamental to be eradicated during three and four generations in America. Our American born Trønders may be full fledged Americans but they have still a Trønder soul.

It is this Trønder soul that we want to save. We want to save it by having the young America Trønders know their inmost self and how it became as it is, in order that they may know how to adjust it to the life they are helping to create in their American homeland.

Furthermore the Trønderlag has endeavored, and hopes to endeavor thereafter, to impress upon its American born generations the value of the spiritual, moral and cultural treasures that their forefathers' people created during their long history in their rugged, stormswept and beautiful Northland, and to calculative and enrich their new homeland with the contributions of mind and hand made by the Norwegian people - their folklore, history, literature, music and whatever else they have of social, political and cultural refinement.

And there is something more to be remembered and treasured: the history, traditions and contributions by our race to American life during the past century, While the Land of the Midnight Sun and its people over there may present a more or less hazy picture to the majority of the third and fourth, and even to the first generation, of American Trønders, the pioneer forefathers and what they did on American soil is definitely present and real in their consciousness. To perpetuate what the pioneers began in building land, homes, business, industry, communities, Church and State, should be a sacred obligation upon their descendants, who now are the heirs of their great American patrimony.

The phase of endeavor has also been cultivated by the Trønderlag of America, and will in a few years be turned over to the American born Trønders to be continued and interpreted to the generations that will follow them.

The time has arrived in America when a person is not honored because he tries to "despise" the racial group from which he sprang, on the contrary, he is honored for loyalty to his own, because this shows character and nobility of soul; fidelity and self-respect, virtues that beget respect for and confidence in that type of person in the minds and hearts of all worthy members of society.

I send out this challenge and appeal to you who are Americans of Trønder stock. Give your pledge that you will carry on when we of the pioneer Trønderlag must relinquish our hold upon the progress of our organization. Step up, young Trønder-Americans! Take hold, and make the idea that carried us through hitherto live and grow and prosper for the honor of the past and the good of the future. Begin now and swing into the movement under the old regime; it will soon be yours to control and maintain.

    Sincerely yours,

        D. G. RISTAD
        1933/1934

Historical List of Stevne Sites & Officers

Fergus Falls, MN - September 17, 1908
President: M. A. Wollan; Vice President: O. C. Hauan; Secretary-Treasurer: S. O. Leirfallom; Board Members: J. N. Kildahl, Thomas Warlow, J. B. Wist, D. G. Ristad, Knut Gjerseth

Glenwood, MN - June 18-19, 1909
President: M. A. Wollan; Vice Presidents: O. M. Oleson, O. C. Hauan, D. C. Jordahl; Secretary-Treasurer: Sivert Leirfallom; Board Members: Consul Wist, Prof. Ristad, Prof. Kindahl, Prof. Gjerseth, Mr. Warloe; Editor: Nicolay Grevstad, Consul Bendeke, Sivert Oksness, C. Christianson

Formand M. A. Wollan of Glenwood, MN

Grand Forks, ND - July 1-2, 1910
President: Ole M. Oleson, Vice Presidents: T. C. Wollan, Konsul Bendeke, Nic Grevstad, J. F. Strass, Pastor Jordahl, Carl Helle, Sivert Oksness, Gunder Winkjer, Prof. C. Christianson, Ole Olson; Secretary-Treasurer: T. C. Wollan; Board Members: M. A. Wollan, J.N. Kildahl, D. G. Ristad, Konsul Johs. B. Wist, T. Warlow, O. M. Hauan, A. C. Floan, L. Hoyseth

Sioux Falls, SD - July 1-2, 1911
President: Ole M. Oleson; Vice Presidents: O. C. Johnson, H. Bendeke, Nicolay Grevstad, J. F. Strass, D. C. Jordahl, Carl Helle, Sivert Oksness, Gunder Winkjer; Secretary-Treasurer: T. C. Wollan; Board Members: D. G. Ristad, Konsul J. B. Wist, T. Warloe, O. M. Hauan, J. N. Kildahl, M. A. Wollan

Minneapolis, MN - June 14-15, 1912
President: Halfdan Bendeke; Vice Presidents: O. C. Johnson, C. T. Wollan, L. L. Masted, Carl Helle, M. O. Sumstad, Knut Lokken, Olaf O. Ray; Secretary-Treasurer: Ingebrigt Dorrum; Board Members: O. M. Olson, D. G. Ristad, T. Warloe, J. N. Kildahl, M. A. Wollan, Ole O. Ydstie

Glenwood, MN - June 6o7, 1913
President Halfdan Bendeke; Vice Presidents: Kasper T. Wollan, L. O. Haug, Lars Hoyseth, Olaf Ray, O. L. Wennes, Bess Paulsness, August Wangberg; Secretary-Treasurer: I. Dorrum; Board Members: T. Warloe, Ole Ydstie, D. G. Ristad, O. M. Oleson, M. A. Wollan, M. O. Sumstad

Minneapolis, MN - May 16-18, 1914
President: Sigurd O. Hanger; Vice Presidents: Casper T. Wollan, L. O. Haug, Lars Hoyseth, Olaf Ray, O.L. Wennes, Bess Paulsness, August Wangberg, John Hogstad, Einar Johnson: Secretary-Treasurer: I. Dorrum; Board Members: D. G. Ristad, O. M. Oleson, M. A. Wollan, M. O. Sumstad, Ole O. Ydstie, Ole Sellness

Konsul Halfdan Bendeke (1869-1915)

Fargo, ND - June 26-27, 1915
President: Sigurd Hanger; Secretary-Treasurer: I. Dorrum; Asst. Secretary: Syvert S. Oksness; Historian: D. G. Ristad; Directors: H. J. Hagen, J. E. Kyllo, N. O. Stageberg, L. W. Pederson, Kasper T. Wollan, Andrew Skarvold, Lars Hoyseth, Olaf Ray, Einar Johnson, Bess Paulsness, L.O. Haug

Willmar, MN - June 24-25, 1916
President: Sigurd Hanger; Vice Presidents: Kasper T. Wollan, L. O. Haug, S. S. Glarum, J. Dahl, Rev. D. C. Jordahl, K. Saugestad, T. J. Alstad; Secretary-Treasurer: I. Dorrum; New Directors: M. A. Wollan, Rev. M. O. Sumstad

Canton, SD - June 21-22, 1917
President: P. M. Glasoe; Secretary-Treasurer: I. Dorrum; Vice Presidents: Bess O. Paulsness, Kasper T. Wollan,

Professor Ingebrigt Dorrum

Trønderlag History

Einer Johnson, Rev. D. C. Jordahl, K. Saugestad, Olaf Ray, J. F. Strass, A. Halseth, Prof. Hegre; Directors: H. J. Hagen, J. E. Kyllo, M. A. Wollan, M. O. Sumstad, Ole N. Ydstie, Ole Selnes

1918 - No Stevne (War)
President: P. M. Glasoe; Secretary-Treasurer: I. Dorrum

Eau Claire, WI - June 25-26, 1919
President: P. M. Glasoe; Vice Presidents: Elling Strand, T. J. Oyaas, Bess O. Paulsness; Secretary-Treasurer: F. L. Trønsdal; Board Members: Mathias Froium, Knute Løkken, Prof. J. G. Halland, Ole Røe

Prof. P. M. Glasoe, Ph.D.
Northfield, MN

Superior, WI - June 24-25, 1920
President: P. M. Glasoe; Vice Presidents: S. S. Joyen, O. S. Amery; Secretary-Treasurer: F. L. Tronsdal; Directors: John Oyaas, H. J. Hagen, J. E. Kyllo, M. O. Sumstad, Tobias Thompson, Ole Silnes; Vice Presidents: B. O. Paulsness, Kasper Volland, O. S. Lie, K. Saugestad, Olaf Ray, J. F. Strass, Prof. Hegre, Sivert Hoyum, A. Halseth.

Grand Forks, ND - June 16-17, 1921
President: P. M. Glasoe; Vice President: B. O. Paulsness; Secretary-Treasurer: W. P. Rognlie; Board Members: John Oyass, J. G. Halland, J. E. Kyllo, M. O. Sumstad, Tobias Thompson, Ole Selness

Sioux Falls, SD - June 20-21, 1922
President: John Alphson; Secretary-Treasurer: W. P. Rognlie

Zumbrota, MN - June 6-7, 1923
President: John Alphson; Secretary-Treasurer: W. P. Rognlie

Madison, MN - June 10-11, 1924
President: Edward Hammer; Secretary-Treasurer: W. P. Rognlie; Board Members: Ole Silness, D. Eliason, O.P. Ojen, Jens Undlin, Fredrik Kavli, John Johnson

Minneapolis/St. Paul, MN - June 6. 1925
President: D. G. Ristad; Sescretary-Treasurer: W. P. Rognlie; Board Members: Ole Silnes, D. Eliason, O. P. Ojen, Jens Undlin, Fredrik Kavli, John Johnson

Duluth, MN - June 11-13, 1926
President: D. G. Ristad; Vice Presidents: Ole P. Borstad, H. O. Hall, Louis Ronning, Mrs. Anna Queber, Lars O. Haug, B. O. Stordahl, Albert Dubvad, John Nornborg, Sam Haugdahl; Secretary-Treasurer: W. P. Rognlie; Board Members: O.P. Ojen, Jens Undlin, Fredrik Kavli, John Johnson, Ole Silnes, D. Eliason

Thief River Falls, MN - July 1-3, 1927
President: D. G. Ristad; Vice President: Lars O. Haug; Secretary: John Nornberg; Treasurer: E. J. Oyen; Historian: O. M. Norlie

Dell Rapids, SD - June 8-10, 1928
President: D. G. Ristad; Secretary: John Nornborg; Treasurer: E. J. Oyan

Decorah, IA - June 7-9, 1929
President: D. G. Ristad; Secretary: John Nornberg

Minneapolis, MN - June 12, 1930
President: D. G. Ristad; Secretary: John Nornborg

Starbuck, MN - June 12-14, 1931
President: D. G. Ristad: Secretary: O. Hegdahl; Treasurer: E. J. Oyan; Jubilee Committee: D. G. Ristad; Lars O. Haug, E. J. Oyan, John Nornborg

Hendricks, MN - June 17-19, 1932
President: D. G. Ristad; Vice President: Lars Haug, J. H. Myrvang; Secretary: O. Hegdahl; Treasurer: E. J. Oyan; Yearbook Editor: John Nornborg

Fergus Falls, MN - August 25-27, 1933
President: D. G. Ristad; Vice Presidents: Lars O. Haug, J. H. Myrwang; Secretary: O. Hegdahl; Treasurer: E. J. Oyan; Aarbok Editor: John Nornborg

Glenwood, MN - June 15-17, 1934
President: D. G. Ristad; Vice Presidents: Lars O. Haug, J. H. Myrwang; Secretary: O. Hegdahl; Treasurer: E. J. Oyan; Editor: John Nornborg

Dell Rapids, SD - 1935
President: W. P. Rognlie; Vice-President: Gerald R. Giving; Secretary O. Hegdahl; Treasurer: E. J. Oyan; Editor: John Nornborg

Madison, MN - 1936
President: W. P. Rognlie; Secretary O. Hegdahl

Duluth, MN - 1937
President J. A. Myrwang; Vice Presidents: Gerold Giving, Hans C. Ness; Secretary: O. Hegdahl; Treasurer: Mrs. H. O. Kirkvold; Editor: John Nornborg

Grand Forks, ND - June 24-26, 1938
President: J. A. Myrwang; Vice President: Hans Ness; Secretary O. Hegdahl; Treasurer: Mrs. H. O. Kirkvold; Historian: John Nornborg; Editor: Mrs. Kristine Haugen

Canton, SD - 1939
President: J. A. Myrwang; Secretary: O. Hegdahl

Zumbrota, MN - 1940
President: J. A. Myrwang; Secretary: O. Hegdahl

Fergus Falls, MN - June 27-29, 1941
President: J. A. Myrwang; Vice President: Henry Nycklemoe; Secretary: O. Hegdahl; Treasurer: Mrs. Olava Kirkvold.

1942 - No Stevne
President: Henry Nycklemoe; Vice President: Ole Hegdahl; Secretary: Elfrida Nervick; Treasurer: Mrs. Olava Kirkvold; Editor: Kristine Haugan

1943 - No Stevne
President: Henry Nycklemoe; Secretary: Elfrida Nervick

Aarbok Editor, John Nornborg

J. A. Myrwang

TRØNDERLAG CENTENNIAL CELEBRATION

1944 - No Stevne
President: Henry Nycklemoe; Secretary: Elfrida Nervick

1945 - No Stevne
President: Henry Nycklemoe; Secretary: Elfrida Nervick

Appleton, MN - June 21-23, 1946
President: Henry Nycklemoe; Secretary: Elfrida Nervick

Bemidji, MN - July 25-27, 1947
President: P. M. Glasoe; Vice President: Ole Hegdahl; Secretary: Elfrida Nervick; Treasurer: Borghild Horjem

Site Unknown - June 3-4, 1948
President: P. M. Glasoe; Secretary: Elfrida Nervick

Duluth, MN - 1949
President: P. M. Glasoe; Secretary: Elfrida Nervick

Minneapolis, MN - June 23-25, 1950
President: P. M. Glasoe; Secretary: Elfrida Nervick

Fargo, ND - June 8-9, 1951
President: Christian Ellingsen; Vice President: Henry Møllendahl; Secretary: Elfrida Nervick; Treasurer: Borghild Horjem

La Crosse, WI - June 20-21, 1952
President: Christian Ellingsen; Secretary: Elfrida Nervick

Grand Forks, ND - June 19-21, 1953
President: O. L. Draveng; Vice President: Ragnvold Gotaas; Secretary: Elfrida Nervick; Treasurer: Borghild Horjem; Editor: O. Hegdahl

Fergus Falls, MN - June 11-12, 1954
President: O. L. Draveng; Vice President: Ragnvold Gotaas; Secretary: Elfrida Nervick; Treasurer: Borghild Horjem; Editor: O. Hegdahl; Financial Sec: A. J. Broback

Devils Lake, ND - June 17-19, 1955
President: O. L. Draveng; Vice President: Ragnvold Gotaas;

Secretary: Elfrida Nervick; Treasurer: Borghild Horjem; Editor: O. Hegdahl

Decorah, IA - June 15-16, 1956
President: O. L. Draveng; Vice President: Ragnvold Gotaas; Secretary: Elfrida Nervick; Treasurer: Borghild Horjem; Editor: O. Hegdahl

Duluth, MN - June 7-9, 1957
President: O. L. Draveng; Vice President: Ragnvold Gotaas; Secretary: Elfrida Nervick; Treasurer: Borghild Horjem; Editor: O. Hegdahl

Fergus Falls, MN - June 6-7, 1958
President: Ragnvald Gotaas, Vice President: Sigurd Alphson; Secretary: Elfrida Nervick; Treasurer Odd Aune; Financial Sec.: Ingeborg Romstad; Editor: O. Hegdahl

Ragnvald Gotaas, Trønderlag President 1958-1962

Thief River Falls, MN - June 12-13, 1959
President: Ragnvald Gotaas; Secretary: Elfrida Nervick

St. Cloud, MN - July 1-2, 1960
President: Ragnvald Gotaas; Secretary: Elfrida Nervick

Minneapolis, MN - June 16-17, 1961
President: Ragnvald Gotaas; Secretary: Elfrida Nervick; Treasurer: Odd L. Aune

Site Unknown - 1962
President: Ragnvald Gotaas; Secretary: Elfrida Nervick

Devils Lake, ND - June 14-15, 1963
President: Henry Nycklemoe; Secretary: Anna Nilsen

Site Unknown - 1964
President: Henry Nycklemoe; Secretary: Anna Nilsen

Minneapolis, MN - June 11-12, 1965
President: Henry Nycklemoe; Secretary: Anna Nilsen

Fergus Falls, MN - June 24-25, 1966
President: Henry Nycklemoe; Vice President: Paul Paulson; Secretary: Elfrida Nervick; Treasurer: Sam Eng

No Trønderlag Stevner - 1967-1979 (Organization disbanded)

Appleton, MN - 1980 (Trønderlag re-organized)
Co-Chairs: Mrs. Berdeen Valla & Mrs. Lowell Oellien; Secretary: Orvin Larson; Treasurer: Ellsworth Smogard; Historian: Mr. & Mrs. Floyd Boraas

Appleton-Dawson-Madison, MN - June 19-21, 1981
Co-Chairs: Mrs. Berdeen Valla & Mrs. Lowell Oellien; Secretary: Orvin Larson; Treasurer: Ellsworth Smogard; Board Members: Ellsworth Smogard, Bernice Oellien, Orvin Larson, Mabel Vaala, Meridith Ulstad, Irene Chapman, Selma Boraas, Curtis Olson, Esther Opoien, Leonard Kirkeby; Historian: Meredith Ulstad

Dawson, MN - June 25-27-1982
Co-Chairs: Mable Vaala & Bernice Oellien; Secretary: Orvin Larson; Treasurer: Ellsworth Smogard; Board Members: Ellsworth Smogard, Orvin Larson, Merideth Ulstad, Selma Boraas, Bernice Oellien, Mabel Vaala, Irene Chapman, Curtis Olson, Esther Opoien, Merideth Ulstad; Historian: Selma Boraas

Fergus Falls, MN - July 15-17, 1983
Co-Chairs: Mable Vaala & Bernice Oellien; Secretary: Orvin Larson; Treasurer: Ellsworth Smogard; Board: Leonard Kirkeby, Curtiss Olson, Esther Opoin, Arlyn Bliss

Appleton, MN - June 22-24, 1984
Co-Chairs: Mable Vaala & Bernice Oellien; Secretary: Orvin Larson; Board Members: Leonard Kirkeby, Eileen Chapman, Mabel Vaala, Esther Opoin, Curtiss Olson, Arlyn Bliss

Rochester, MN - June 14-16, 1985
Co-Chairs: Mable Vaala & Bernice Oellien; Board Members: Curtis Olson, Esther Opoien

Dawson, MN - June 27-29, 1986
Co-Chairs: Mable Vaala & Bernice Oellien; Secretary: Orvin Larson; Board Members: Oliver Nypan, Gary Flatgard, Selma Boraas

TRØNDERLAG HISTORY

Mankato, MN - July 17-18, 1987
President: Gary Flatgard; Vice President: Bernice Oellien; Secretary Arlyn Bliss; Treasurer: Selma Boraas; Board Members: Ollie Nypan, Alf Swenson, Arlene Skjei, James Pederson, Orvin Larson, Selma Boraas; Genealogist: James Pederson; Historian: Orvin Larson

Fargo, ND - July 22-12, 1988
President: Gary Flatgard; Vice President: Mike Miller; Secretary: Arlyn Bliss; Treasurer: Myrtle Kolstad; Board Members: Oliver B. Nypan, Allison Breiwick, Mike Miller, Palmer Paulson, Myrtle Kolstad; Historian: Arlene Skjei; Genealogist: James Pederson

Gary Flatgard, Trønderlag president from 1987-1991 and 1996-2002

Fergus Falls, MN - June 16-17, 1989
President: Gary Flatgard; Vice President: Mike Miller; Secretary: Arlyn Bliss; Treasurer: Myrtle Kolstad; Board Members: Oliver B. Nypan, Aileen Torrence, Allison Breiwick, Yvonne Marts; Editor: Caroline Breiwick; Genealogist: James Pederson; Historian: Arlene Skjei

Madison, MN - June 21-22, 1991
President: Gary Flatgard; Vice President: Caroline Breiwick; Secretary: Yvonne Marts; Treasurer: Myrtle Kolstad; Board Members: Oliver B. Nypan, Allison Breiwick, Harold Hanson, Aileen Torrence; Editor: Caroline Breiwick; Historian: Harold Hanson; Genealogist: James Pederson

Willmar, MN - June 26-27, 1992
President: Yvonne Marts; Vice President: Caroline Breiwick; Secretary: Aileen Torrence; Treasurer: Myrtle Kolstad; Board Members: Olga Westmoe, Kenneth Brekke, Bernice Oellien, Jan Worel; Historian: Allison Breiwick; Genealogist: James Pederson; Editor: Caroline Breiwick

Montevideo, MN - June 25-26, 1993
President: Yvonne Marts; Vice President: Bernice Oellien; Secretary: Aileen Torrence; Treasurer: Alice Brask; Board Members: Olga Westmoe, Barry Dahl, Kenneth Brekke, Arlyn

Bliss, Roland Krogstad; Historian: Kenneth Brekke; Genealogist: James Pederson

Rochester, MN - June 24-25, 1994
President: Yvonne Marts; Vice President: Bernice Oellien; Secretary: Aileen Torrence; Treasurer: Alice Brask; Board Members: Barry Dahl, Ralph Larson, Clifford Hoff, Palmer Paulson; Historian: Kenneth Brekke; Genealogist: James Pederson

Montevideo, MN - June 23-24, 1995
President: Clifford Hoff; Vice President: Bernice Oellien; Secretary: Aileen Torrence; Treasurer: Alice Brask; Board Members: Yvonne Marts, Ralph Larson, Barry Dahl, Palmer Paulson; Historian: Kenneth Brekke; Genealogist: James Pederson

Sioux Falls, SD - August 16-17, 1996
President: Clifford Hoff; Vice President: Bernice Oellien; Secretary: Aileen Torrence; Treasurer: Alice Brask; Board Members: Mary Benson, Ralph Larson, Everett Kolstad, Palmer Paulson; Historian: Kenneth Brekke; Genealogist: James Pederson & Barry Dahl

Decorah, IA - August 15-16, 1997
President: Gary Flatgard; Vice President: Palmer Paulson; Secretary: Aileen Torrence; Treasurer: Alice Brask; Board Members: Mary Benson, Bernice Oellien, Everett Kolstad; Historian: Kenneth Brekke; Genealogist: James Pederson & Barry Dahl

Mankato, MN - July 31-August 1, 1998
President: Gary Flatgard; Vice President: Palmer Paulson; Secretary: Mary Benson; Treasurer: Alice Brask; Board Members: John Grindberg, Larry Thompson, Barry Dahl, Everett Kolstad, Ardell Myran; Genealogist: James Pederson & Barry Dahl

Plymouth, MN - September 24-25, 1999
President: Gary Flatgard; Vice President: Palmer Paulson; Secretary: Ann Duff; Treasurer: John Grindberg; Board

Trønderlag History

Members: Barry Dahl, Dorothy Mikkelson, Ardell Myran, Eunice Quamen, Larry Thompson; Historian: Ardell Myran; Editor: Eunice Quamen; Genealogist: Barry Dahl

Granite Falls, MN - September 22-23, 2000
President: Gary Flatgard; Vice President: Larry Thompson; Secretary: Dorothy Mikkelson; Treasurer: Eunice Quamen; Board Members: Barry Dahl, Herbert Mikkelson, Ardell Myran, John Grindberg; Genealogist: Barry Dahl; Editor: Eunice Quamen

Starbuck, MN - August 9-11, 2001
President: Gary Flatgard; Vice President: Larry Thompson; Secretary: Dorothy Mikkelson; Treasurer: Eunice Quamen; Board Members: Barry Dahl, Herbert Mikkelson, Ardell Myran, Francis Myran, Linda Schwartz; Genealogist: Barry Dahl; Historian: Ardell Myran; Editor: Linda Schwartz

2001 Board Meeting in Starbuck, MN

St. Paul, MN - August 9-12, 2002
President: Gary Flatgard; Vice President: Larry Thompson; Secretary: Dorothy Mikkelson; Treasurer: Herbert Mikkelson; Board Members: Barry Dahl, Marcia Hansen, Johanna Hocker, Linda Schwartz, Ardell Myran, Francis Myran; Editor & Webmaster: Linda Schwartz; Historian: Ardell Myran; Genealogist: Barry Dahl

Sioux Falls, SD - August 6-9, 2003 (First Tre Lag Stevne)
President: Linda Schwartz; Vice President: Johanna Hocker; Secretary: Marcia Hanson; Treasurer: Elaine Hasleton; Board Members: Terry Brende, Ardell Myran; Francis Myran; Palmer Paulson; Kathleen Sturre; Editor & Webmaster: Linda Schwartz; Genealogist: Barry Dahl

Rochester, MN - August 4-7, 2004
President: Linda Schwartz; Vice President: Johanna Hocker; Secretary: Marcia Hansen; Treasurer: Terry Brende; Board

Members: Elaine Hasleton, Kathleen Sturre, John Andrisen, Palmer Paulson; Editor & Webmaster: Linda Schwartz; Historian: John Andrisen; Genealogist: Barry Dahl

Fargo, ND - August 3-6, 2005
President: Linda Schwartz; Vice President: Elaine Hasleton; Secretary: Marcia Hansen; Treasurer: Terry Brende; Board Members: Robert Moffett, Doris Moffett, Kathleen Sturre, John Andrisen; Genealogist: Barry Dahl; Historian: John Andrisen; Editor & Webmaster: Linda Schwartz

Eau Claire, WI - August 2-5, 2006
President: Linda Schwartz; Vice President: Elaine Hasleton; Secretary: Marcia Hansen; Treasurer: Terry Brende; Board Members: Barry Dahl, Robert Moffett, Doris Moffett, John Andrisen, Nancy Hawkinson; Historian John Andrisen; Genealogist: Barry Dahl; Editor & Webmaster: Linda Schwartz

Linda Schwartz, Trønderlag President 2003-2008

Onalaska, WI - August 1-4, 2007
President: Linda Schwartz; Vice President: Elaine Hasleton; Secretary: Marcia Hansen; Treasurer: Robert Fossum; Board Members: John Andrisen, Gene Hanson, Doris Moffett, Robert Moffett, Patti Goke, Nancy Hawkinson; Genealogist: Barry Dahl; Editor & Webmaster: Linda Schwartz; Historian: John Andrisen; Membership Chair: Gene Hanson; Centennial Chair: Elaine Hasleton

Fergus Falls, MN - August 6-9, 2008
President: Linda Schwartz; Vice President: Elaine Hasleton; Secretary: Nancy Hawkinson; Treasurer: Robert Fossum; Board Members: Barry Dahl, Doris Moffett, Robert Moffett, Oddgeir Fossli, Patricia Peterson, Jon Satrum; Genealogist: Barry Dahl; Editor & Webmaster: Linda Schwartz; Centennial Chair: Elaine Hasleton

South St. Paul, MN - Coming in August 2009

Bygdelags

What Is a Bygdelag?

The "bygdelag" was a social phenomenon of Norwegian immigrants who established and maintained organizations in their new world that were based on geographic communities in the old. A "bygd" is a place or community. A "lag" is an association or organization.

Norwegian immigrants to the United States came largely from rural areas in Norway. Uprooted from the security of their native society, they reorganized their lives, restructured old institutions and created new ones. The bygdelag societies attempted to perpetuate intimate and cherished aspects of Norwegian heritage, including their dialects. These organizations revealed a strong attachment to old country localities, to distinct scenic features and to regional traditions and values.

Bygdelags organize gatherings, or stevner, usually in the summer. They publish newsletters to help members keep in touch. Often featured at a stevne are Norwegian social and cultural activities as well as arts and crafts, books and readings, music, genealogy workshops, noted speakers and visiting people from each specific group's place of origin. The bygdelag help in tracing ancestry and may also organize occasional tours to Norway.

ABOVE: Cousins Joanne Englund and Margie Jokinen shared the experience of visiting their family farm on the Trønderlag Heritage Tour to Norway in September 2005.

A bygd is to be understood as a particular community, group of communities, a general district or fjord region or valley. The strongest loyalty of the organizers was toward the place where a person was more comfortable. The establishment of the bygdelags was an intentionally conservative movement aimed at maintaining feelings and cultural memories that seemed to be fading.

The first bygdelag was organized by immigrants from Valdres who held their first meeting in Minnehaha Park in Minneapolis 25 June 1899. In 1907 lags were organized for Telelaget and Hallinglaget. Four new bygdelags were established in 1908: Sognalaget, Trønderlaget, Nordlandslaget and Numedalslaget. Later about 20 more lags were founded. Today there are approximately 32 bygdelags in existence.

All bygdelags have several things in common, among them the celebration of Norwegian nature and the honoring of the work and sacrifices that had to be made in the early days of settlement.

The year 1925 marked an important milestone in bygdelag history. When the twin cities, St. Paul and Minneapolis, celebrated a century of Norwegian immigration, the bygdelags were the organizers of the impressive celebration. The event emphasized the Viking discover of America and President Coolidge, who was in attendance, acknowledged the Norwegian wish to be recognized as the discoverer of America. The pioneer history was also emphasized.

Further information about the various bygdelags can be obtained through the Bygdelagenes Fellesraad, a national council headed by President Marilyn D. Somdahl. See their web site at http://www.fellesraad.com or write to Marilyn Somdahl at 5100 West 102 St #209, Minneapolis, MN 55437

Based on "The Bygdelag: A Norwegian Phenomenon" from *News of Norway*, Issue 5, 1996.

The Land of a Thousand Lakes

(Source: *Den Siste Folkevandring Sagastubber fra Nybyggerlivet i Amerika*, by Hjalmar Rued Holand, 1930; *Norwegians in America: The Last Migration*, by Hjalmar Rued Holand, translated by Helmer M. Blegen, 1978, pp. 191–196. Used with permission of Deb Nelson Gourley, Astri My Astri)

There was a time long, long ago when Manitou, the good creator of the red man, walked about on earth. As he was looking at his creation to see how his children were getting along, he noticed that his red sons at the feet of the Rocky Mountains were languishing. Only rarely did the refreshing rains fall from the heavens, so the grass withered and the deer were seen no more. The few lakes remaining held only bitter, salty waters; and it was a long, long walk to the cool, fresh springs.

Then Manitou took up an old water bag that he had not used since he created the world, and he carried it to the big inland sea that people now call Lake Superior. This lake is filled with the world's purest and tastiest water, issuing from the thousand eternal springs. There, he filled his water bag to bring water to his thirsty children in the Far West.

But the water bag was old and fragile, and once in a while big drops leaked out and fell to the ground. These became shiny lakes, twinkling pearls on the broad bosom of Minnesota.

When Manitou got as far as the high land that people call Otter Tail County, the bag burst, thus forming hundreds of delightful lakes. The water, clear and cold, flowed out of these lakes and gathered into big rivers. One river flows east and one flows west. One river flows north to the darkness of the sea of ice, and another river flows south to the steamy sea where the palm trees grow.

Then Manitou noticed that he had come to the middle point of the world, the ancient Paradise from which rivers flow in different directions. This, one can still read in the books of the palefaces.

And Manitou looked, and he saw that the place on which he stood was very beautiful, and so he said: "Why should I carry water to my children in the Far West, where only the cactus and the rattlesnake thrive? My sons are young and strong. Let them come here where there is much game, billowing plains and great woods, where there are lakes with many, many fish, and a very beautiful land."

And Manitou opened wide his mouth and called with a powerful voice. The red children of the Far West heard his call, and they came, and they found great joy when they beheld the beauty of the land.

Norwegians Rule in Otter Tail County

Otter Tail County is a mighty county. It is about as large in area as the state of Delaware, which has a governor, senators, state graft and corruption, and obscenity.

These last things are not found here, for it is the Norwegian who here reigns with wisdom and power.

The county has a population of about 47,000, of which nearly half are Norwegian in origin. The southern and western parts of the county are especially fertile, and here the Norwegians are in uncontested control. With the exception of Polk County, Minnesota, no other county in the U.S. has a greater Norwegian population.

Otter Tail County's Norwegian history goes back to the year 1867. Down in the southeast corner of Minnesota, about where the little town of Mabel is located, there were, in 1866, many Trønderne and others who wanted to go west to look for land. In the vicinity of Mabel, the land was already too high in price for them to buy.

Being inexperienced in the matter of land-seeking, they agreed among themselves to send out a couple of capable and experienced men to discover a region that offered the best possibilities for the founding of a new colony and had promise for the future. A dozen men chipped in $5 each, and they selected Nils Wollan and Ole Aasved, both from Stod near Trondheim.

Nils Wollan was a very knowledgeable man of a certain particular nature that bordered on the traditional Trønderne stubbornness. Ole Aasved was also an intelligent man of long experience in America. He had been here since 1850 and was the actual leader of emigration from the Trondheim district. They were, thus, two fine fellows—strong, daring and persevering. They were just what was required to undertake such a difficult and risky journey.

The two men headed toward the north and west and examined the land in an area 300 miles long, until they reached Fort Pomme de Terre, an old frontier fort in the northeast corner of Grant County. From here they set their course straight southward through a half-score of still quite unoccupied counties in western Minnesota. They slept outside at night, waded or swam across great rivers and lived on what their rifles could provide them.

They continued onward across the naked wastes of Iowa, where all they saw was an occasional pioneer shanty, until they reached the village of Des Moines in southern Iowa. From there they headed northeast, traversed the whole state of Iowa and returned to Mabel. They had been gone about two months and had made the whole distance of 1,100 miles on foot.

When they were to deliver their report on their travels, a large audience was present to hear what Nils Wollan and Ole Aasved had to say. Their account was followed by a long discussion. The final outcome of all these activities was that a group of 18 men, almost all of them Trønderne, decided to accompany Nils Wollan to northwestern Minnesota, while three men went with Ole Aasved to southern Iowa. Another company of nine men, mostly Sogninger, resolved to follow Wollan, but they traveled in a separate expedition.

At the end of May 1867, Wollan and his company started out with many wagons, oxen, cows, pigs, chickens, household goods and many other things. It was a large and substantial caravan that hereby set out to push the milestone of civilization's frontier a hundred miles farther out into the wilderness.

The old-timers remembered the summer of 1867 as the rainiest summer in history. One rainstorm came directly after the other. The level plains turned into lakes, and every low place and swampy depression became a deep lake. Tiny brooks grew to the proportions of mighty rivers, and the larger water- courses became rushing floods. The few bridges were washed away, and the wheels of wagons sank, deeply and heavily, into the water-soaked ground.

This was the kind of weather and road conditions that the company experienced on its trek to its unknown destination, 300 miles away. Many times it seemed a hopeless undertaking to attempt a crossing over the foaming stretches of lowlands; but a man from Østerdal, Ole Lillemoen, soon earned recognition for being the most skillful and competent navigator of the company. He proved to be so resourceful that he could master the most difficult of situations.

At the Zumbro River, the current was extremely strong and broad. Here they removed the wagon boxes and ran chains through the eye, or loop, at the end of the bolsters of the wagons. Then they placed the boxes back on the wagons so that they rested higher on the vehicle than before.

Having secured the strong chains to keep the wagon box firm, they placed the women and children on top of the piles of bedding and pillows in the wagon box. Then they hitched 16 oxen to each wagon and drove them into the stream. The drivers, clinging to the horns of the oxen, waded and swam beside them to guide them across.

Each unit was composed of a long string of oxen pulling a wagon on which sat, precariously perched on high, the women and children. The wagons reeled from side to side, but as soon as the lead oxen felt their feet touch the ground, the strong-legged animals easily pulled the wagon safely up on land. Then the 16 oxen were unhitched and driven back to the other side, and the same process was repeated until all the wagons were safely brought to the opposite shore.

From here the caravan resumed its journey to St. Paul, Minneapolis and St. Cloud. Now they were entering the mysterious unknown of the wild territory, and here all that they saw were Indians and sometimes a solitary hunter.

They drove across the counties of Stearns, Pope, Douglas and Grant, at that time unpopulated, quiet and empty. They saw many places that seemed very beautiful and promising, but there was always someone who found one objection or other, since there were so many kinds of personalities in this large group.

An air of Old Testament noble grandeur prevailed about these pathfinders who were so boldly moving toward a land of promise so far out in the unknown remoteness. It must have been like this when Abraham and his people in the dawn of history walked far to the west to find new land.

It was not only need that urged them onward. Essentially, it was the burning flame of a creative urge deep within their being, the strongest and best motivating power that all human creatures carry inside them, whether conscious of it or not.

They had cattle, large and small, plows, tools, seeds for planting and many children. Now they were advancing, undaunted, defying all opposition and eager to work hard in order to build a new kingdom.

When they eventually reached Pomme de Terre, the fort at the most northern point visited by Nils Wollan on his voyage of discovery, he and several others did not want to go any farther. With a few other Trønderne men, Wollan went back to Pope County, where they laid the foundation for the big Trønderne colony north of Starbuck. Gradually, eight of the Wollan brothers settled here and, in time, became the progenitors of a populous tribe of Wollans in the county.

The other half of the large company went on north to Otter Tail County. Here they also found, only a couple of hours from Pomme de Terre, a fascinatingly beautiful and fertile stretch of country.

They settled east and west of Dalton, a town named after Ole Dahl. This town is in St. Olaf Township, which is not surpassed by any township in the state in fertility or beauty of the surroundings.

Blue Mounds Township

The following information comes from Blue Mounds Historical Society documents and from the book Builders of Pope County by Daisy Ellen Hughes (1930):

The first to settle Pope County's Blue Mounds Township in 1867 were Rasmus Olsen Signalness, his wife, Bergitte Stolsdoken Signalness, and their family.

Rasmus was born at Ophem-Lien, Nord Torpe, Buskerud fylke. Bergitte was born on Blegtved farm near Gol, Hallingdal, Buskerud fylke. They were married at Gol. Rasmus and Bergitte lived on Signaldalen, Nordland, before coming to the U.S. in 1862.

For the next five years, the family lived in Dane County and then at Colfax, Dunn County, Wisconsin. They moved to their homestead in Blue Mounds Township, Minnesota, in 1867.

The following 11 children were born to Rasmus and Bergitte: Ole Signalness, Olaus Signalness, Thore Signalness, Gustav Signalness, Anton Signalness, Marie Signalness, Gurine Signalness, Rasmus Signalness, Bertin Signalness, Caroline Signalness and Ole Martin Signalness. Their first winter in Minnesota, Rasmus and Bergitte lived in a dugout near a creek among the trees. They had an Indian family for neighbors, and the Indians taught Rasmus and his family how to survive in the wilderness.

In 1868 and 1869, the following settled in Blue Mounds Township:

- Peter E. Barsness
- Engebret Thompson
- Thomas E. Thompson
- Ole Skaarden
- Peter Svendsrud
- Ole Haugen
- Svend Olson Kaus
- Ole Hagestuen
- Isaac Engebretson
- Andrew L. Brevig
- Cornelius Berg
- Hans Johnshoy

Times were tough for the new settlers in those early years. Luckily, their cows provided them with milk, while the surrounding woods and lakes contained an abundance of wild game and fish. For cash, they turned to trapping, while others worked in the pineries in northern Minnesota. Their oxen furnished them with power and transportation. When these new families needed caulking for their log homes, the Signalness family burned limestone to create lime, an ingredient in plaster.

The nearest market was at St. Cloud, about 90 miles away from the Signalness farm. Olaus would sometimes travel on skies or by oxen to get supplies. From this point he would transport supplies to Fort Abercrombie in northern Dakota Territory.

Once, when he delivered his merchandise, he was cheated on his payment. A large man with a temper, he soon made it clear he was a man to respect. He got his money!

In 1873, Olaus traveled to Benson, Minnesota, to visit some acquaintances. While there, a snowstorm hit. Despite warnings from his friends, Olaus started for home, about 20 miles away. The storm intensified, making travel all but impossible. Olaus found an abandoned shelter for his oxen, but the roof soon caved in from the weight of the snow, forcing them to move on.

While crossing a river north of Benson, the rig broke through the ice, dumping the box off the sleigh runners. Olaus finally managed to get the box back on the runners. He then crawled into the box, letting the oxen have their heads. The oxen followed the snow-packed yet familiar trail, halting when they came to the place of a family acquaintance named Benson. There, Olaus and his team took shelter until the storm let up.

Besides being a farmer, Rasmus held the following positions in Starbuck: assessor, supervisor, school clerk and postmaster. The fine oak log home he built for his family—the oldest house in Pope County—stood for a hundred years. Part of the land was later donated by a grandson to present-day Glacial Ridge Park near Starbuck.

Few towns with Norwegian names

Although the Norwegian pioneers were the first to set a plow in the ground in almost every region they settled in Minnesota and Dakota, there are, nevertheless, only a few place names to commemorate their conquest.

The chief explanation for this is that these old pioneers were a rather modest lot. They even thought it a presumption to burden the English language with such strange names as Torger and Lars, so they humbly allowed themselves to be addressed as Tom and Louis. It was, therefore, an unthinkable monstrosity to impose upon an American landscape the name reminiscent of Norway.

Even when Norwegians almost exclusively populated a township, they waited until some quick-tongued Yankee proposed that the township be named York or Utica in honor of his birthplace. This pliant yielding was a natural consequence of the many years of subjugation to which the Norwegian husmann class had been subjected in the social classification of Norway's population.

However, this general criticism does not apply to Otter Tail County, for in this county there are many Norwegian names: Aastad, Aurdal, Dalton, Folden, Henning, Norman, Nidaros, Norwegian Grove, Oscar, St. Olaf, Sverre, Sverdrup, Stod, Tordenskjold, Trondheim and Weggeland.

It was a Valdris by the name of Ole Jørgensen who was enterprising enough to get most of these monuments to his countrymen placed on the map. He established his home at Wall Lake, east of Fergus Falls, in 1868. In 1869 he was elected to the office of county auditor. This gave him considerable standing and the opportunity to place Norwegian names on many parts of the county.

Two Norwegian centers

From the beginning, Otter Tail County had two focal centers, or points of departure, from which the Norwegian settlers spread out on its extensive areas. The first and the largest of these was the Trønderne settlement in the southern part of the county, the origin of which has been briefly mentioned. The second settlement was Norwegian Grove in the northwest corner of the county. It was started the year after, in 1868, and soon spread over several townships until there now are 12 Norwegian congregations in this part of the county.

From there the Norwegian communities continue without interruption for more than a hundred miles up through the counties of Becker, Clay, Norman and Polk.

To get to Norwegian Grove, when one does not travel by automobile, one changes trains in Fergus Falls. From here there is a small branch line about 20 miles north through a beautiful countryside up to Pelican Rapids.

All around lie Norwegian settlements in every direction, but especially toward the west. Five or six miles away is the old Norwegian Grove, a patch of woods several miles across. Inside these woods is a nice little lake about three miles long called St. Olaf Lake, because there was an Ole living at either end of the lake.

The first settlers built their homes around this grove. Before them, they had the rich billowing prairie and, behind the houses, the protection of the woods. A short distance inside was the lake, with an abundance of fish in it. What more ideal a setting could one desire? To the old pioneers who had come from a rocky and soil-stingy home, this must have seemed like a paradise.

The old pioneers were not blind to the glory, both practical and poetic, that spread out before them when they looked out upon the virgin plain of meadowland on which they had chosen sites for homesteads. Many of them have told of the great lift to the soul they experienced when admiring this Canaan.

It took several years before the pioneers enjoyed any returns from their lands. They lived more like hunters than like agriculturists. They lived so far from any market that it was impossible for them to sell their products.

When they first came here, in 1867, there was no railroad nearer than St. Cloud, 150 miles away. The Great Northern Railway, which now cuts through Otter Tail County, was not built until 12 years later.

Even after the railway came to them, it took a long time for the farmer to realize any profits. The freight rates were so high, as was the cost of the elevators, that the hard-working pioneer had nothing left for himself after so much labor.

The first railway companies, which built their roads under extremely difficult economic conditions, were constantly short of funds, and they took advantage of every possible way to make some money. Their first, and most important, step was to bribe the legislators. For many years, this was a public scandal. By this means, the railroads became free agents and could rob the pioneers as much as they desired.

Farms, churches dot landscape

Otter Tail County, with its thousands of ever-fresh lakes, has an idyllic landscape. Lakes are there in all sizes, from the tiniest duck pond to small seas where the waves can roll for a half score miles before striking the shore.

The circle of fine, stately farm homes in this area are reminiscent of Swedish author Selma Lagerløf's descriptions of Løfvensjø in Vermland. Only the ancient traditions are lacking. There is no recounting of the tale of Gøsta Berling's riding to wild adventures at the head of his 12 cavaliers, nor of any love story about the fair Ingeborg and her Frithiof. There are no memorial monoliths to commemorate the tragic duels of proud knights or the eternal sleep of weary, heroic warriors.

Who can say that the shades and spirits of such ancient heroes do not hover over these waters? It is quite possible that if the Indians had had their poet, their Homer, we might then read, even here, about individuals who could rival those of the half-barbaric Grecian antiquity in heroism and nobility and in great exploits.

But even if this place lacks the magical veil of romanticism that clings to every Norwegian rock and promontory in sacred peace, it nevertheless possesses mementos that give testimony of a better and truer type of struggle and triumph.

Five thousand splendid Norwegian homes, with their cultivated fields and green meadows, tell the story of the pioneer's triumphant battle and conquest of the primordial wilderness. Fifty Norwegian churches testify to his hope in a realm above.

From hill to hill, church spires greet one another across intervening space and their bells ring out, deep-voiced and melodiously: "Glory to God on high! And on earth, peace, good will toward men!"

Reprinted with permission of Deb Nelson Gourley, Astri My Astri Publishing, 602 3rd Ave SW, Waukon, Iowa 52172 USA

Otter Tail County, Minnesota in 1908

According to the *Fergus Falls Journal* on April 8, 1908, the state board of immigration has issued a booklet setting forth the advantages of the various counties of the state. Its description of Otter Tail county is as follows:

Otter Tail county was organized March 18. 1858. The soil is a rich, dark loam and sandy loam with a clay subsoil. The surface is rolling prairie, interspersed with groves of timber, and is traversed by the Red Otter Tail, Leaf and several other rivers, These, with the numerous lakes, for which the county and state are noted, form a perfect drainage system for the county.

Nearly every township in the county has one or more beautiful lakes where the sportsman will find all kinds of fish, while the timbered tracts abound with game.

The area of the county is 2,240.2 square miles or 1,488,726.44 acres of which 1,270,977.77 acres are land and 168,748.62 acres are water. The land surface is divided into 6,227 farms at an average value per acre of $22.72.

Dairying, livestock, poultry and fruit raising are carried on extensively in this county. In 1906 the county had 19 creameries with an output of 1,908,88 lbs. of butter. It also had 7 cheese factories, the output of which was 878,458 lbs. of cheese. The livestock in the county in 1907 was: horses, 21,385; cattle 60,591; sheep 15,941; swine 18,074.

Nearly every home in the county is supplied with rural free delivery and local and long distance telephone. It also has 15 newspapers, 258 rural schools, 11 graded schools, a high school and 76 churches. The population of the county in 1906 was 48,229 of which 5,140 were Norwegian born and 33,759 were American born.

- Information from Fergus Falls Daily Journal, April 8, 1908, page 2

Charter Members

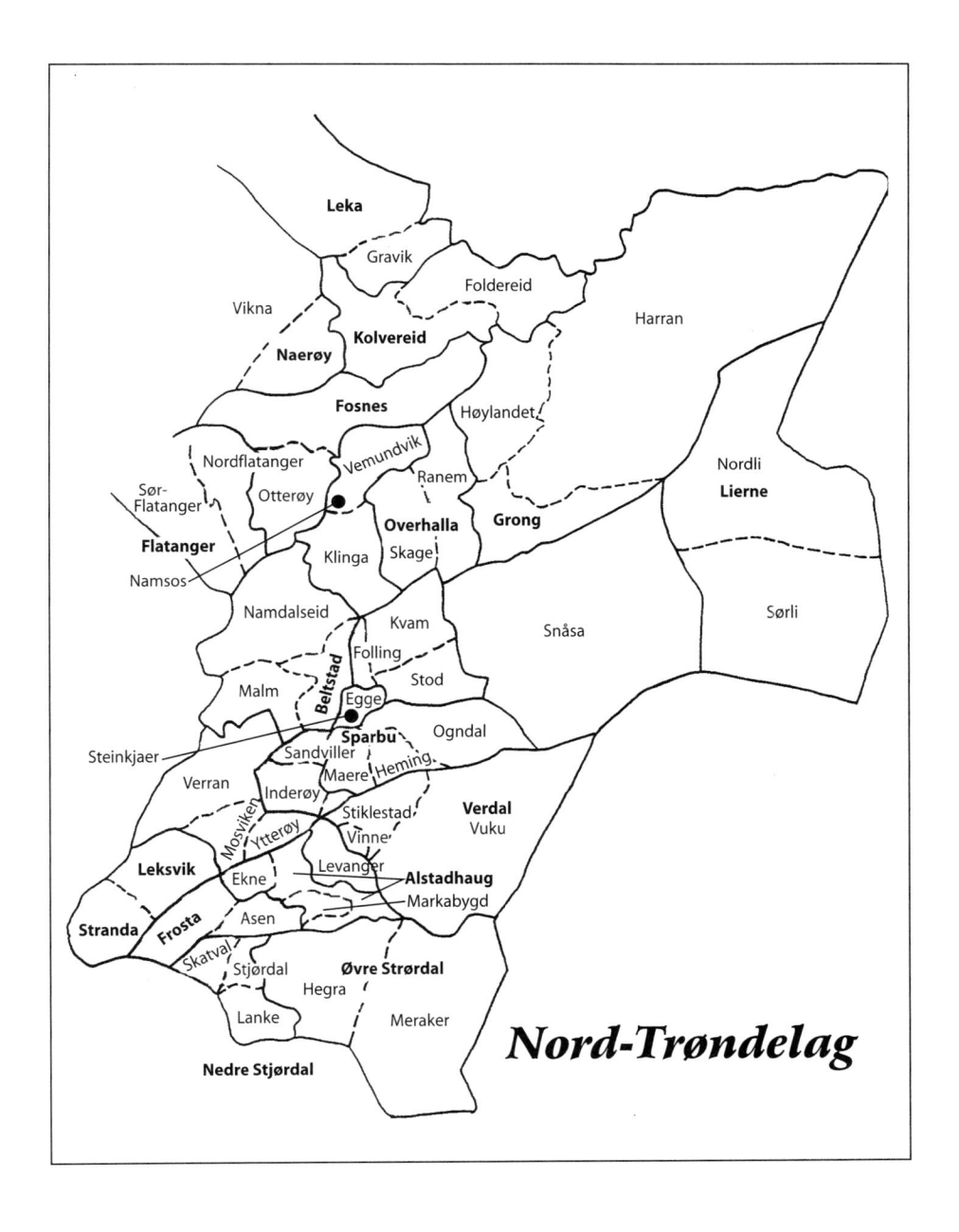

Nord-Trøndelag

Trønderlag Centennial Celebration

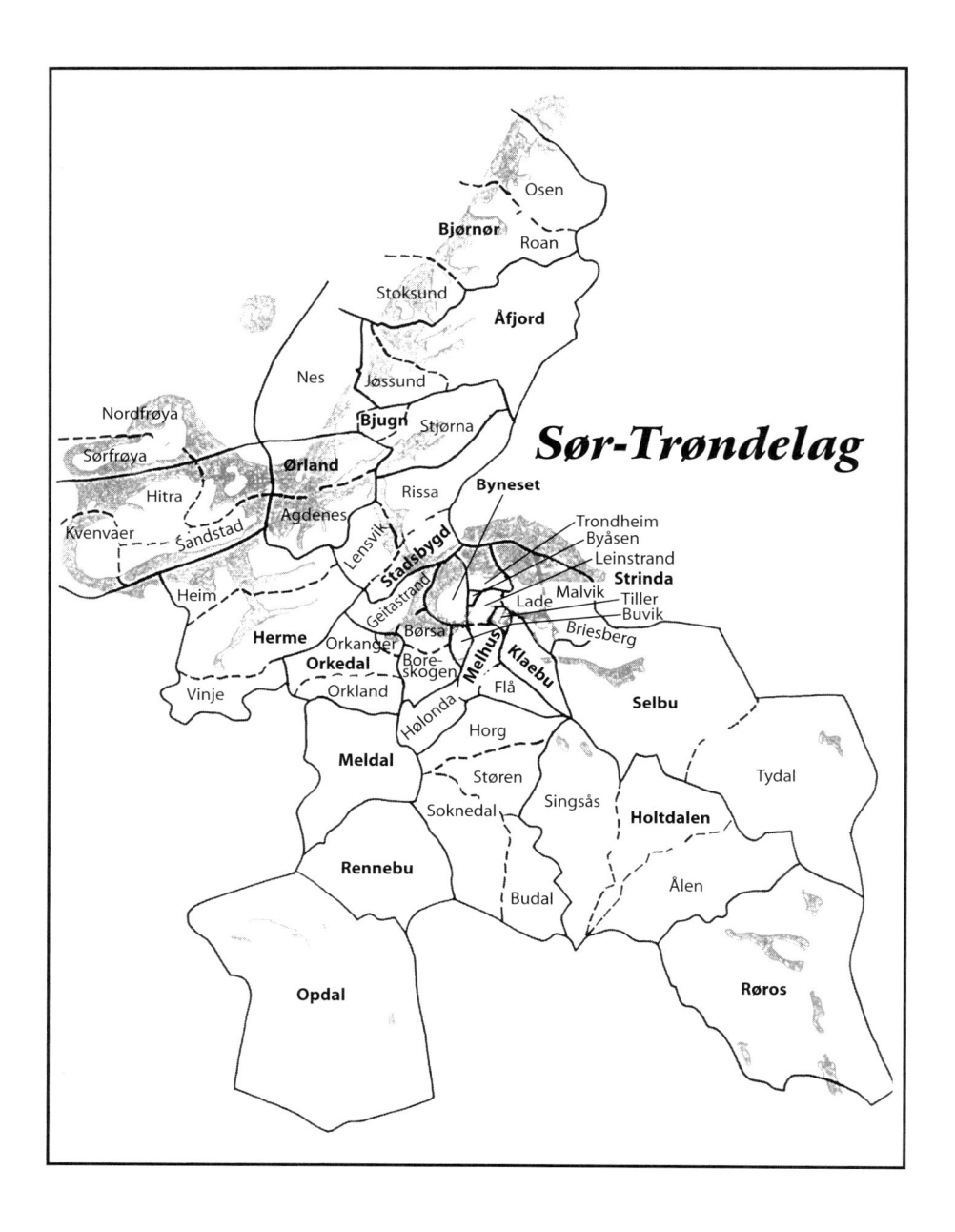

Sør-Trøndelag

CHARTER MEMBERS

Current Trøndelag Kommuner

Sør-Trøndelag	Nord-Trøndelag
Agdenes /Selbekken	**Flatanger** /Lauvsnes
Bjugn /Botngård	**Fosnes** /Dun
Frøya /Sistranda	**Frosta** /Frosta
Hemne /Kyrksæterøra	**Grong** /Grong
Hitra /Fillan	**Høylandet** /Høylandet
Holtålen /Ålen	**Inderøy** / Staumen
Klæbu /Klæbu	**Leka** /Leka
Malvik /Hommelvik	**Leksvik** / Leksvik
Meldal /Meldal	**Levanger** /Levanger
Melhus /Melhus	**Lierne** /Nordli
Midtre Gauldal /Støren	**Meråker** /Meråker
Oppdal /Oppdal	**Mosvik** /Mosvik
Orkdal /Orkanger	**Namsdalseid** /Namdalseid
Osen /Steinsdalen	**Namsos** /Namsos
Rennebu /Berkåk	**Namsskogan** /Namsskogan
Rissa /Rissa	**Nærøy** /Kolvereid
Roan /Roan	**Overhalla** /Overhalla
Røros /Røros	**Røyrvik** /Limingen
Selbu /Selbu	**Snåsa** /Snåsa
Skaun /Børsa	**Steinkjer** /Steinkjer
Snillfjord /Krokstadøra	**Stjørdal** / Stjørdal
Trondheim /Trondheim	**Verdal** /Verdal
Tydal /Tydal	**Verran** /Malm
Ørland / Brekstad	**Vikna** /Rørvik
Åfjord /Årnes	

Note: The Kommune name above is followed by the name of the administrative center for the kommune.

A Few Facts About Charter Members

We found it interesting to note that in 1908 the majority of Charter Members came from Nord-Trøndelag. This is probably related to the number of North Trønders who settled in Minnesota, especially in the Otter Tail County and northern portion of Minnesota.

Of the 120 Charter Members of Trønderlag of America in 1908, 70 percent came from Nord-Trøndelag, 22.5 percent came from Sør-Trøndelag and less than 8 percent came from other parts of Norway – mostly from Mor og Romsdal (places that were part of Trøndelag at one time). Then there were a few who indicated they were from Nord-Trøndelag but were born in other areas and had migrated to Trøndelag to live before they emigrated. Eleven of the Charters Members were born in America after their parents had immigrated.

In the search for descendant families, it was discovered that a number of living people are descendants of more than one Charter Member. A number of Charter Members were siblings or cousins. Some were in-laws.

Charter Member Statistics

Immigration Year

Year	Percent
pre-1865	3%
1865-1869	28%
1870-1879	16%
1880-1889	34%
1890-1899	14%
1900-1908	5%

Charter Members of Trønderlaget of America 1908-09

Name	1908 Residence	Home area	Farm name	Emig.
Martin Aalberg	Henning, MN	Sparbu - NT	Aalberg	1881
C.L. Aanes	Fergus Falls, MN	Beitstaden - NT		1861
Ingebrigt H. Aune	Fergus Falls, MN	Melhus - ST		1882
Nicolai Baglo	Fergus Falls, MN	Verdalen – NT	Baglovald	1886
Carl P. Bye	Fergus Falls, MN	Verdalen – NT	Storøen	1880
Hans Bye	Fergus Falls, MN	Verdalen – NT	Maritvoldvald	1882
Johs. E. Bye	Fergus Falls, MN	Verdalen – NT	Byvald	1886
J.M. Bye	Fergus Falls, MN	Verdalen – NT	Maritvoldvald	1874
B.C. Dahl	Dalton, MN	Beitstad - NT		1866
Gunder Dahl	Fergus Falls, MN	Steinkjer - NT		1866
I. Dorrum	Fergus Falls, MN	Opdal - ST		1899
Ole Ecker	Cloquet, MN	Overhalden - NT	Skage	1882
Ole Eidem	Watson, MN	Frænen – MoR	Eidem	1871
O.P. Einan	Carlisle, MN	Selbu – ST	Einan	1899
Per Ekker	Underwood, MN	Overhalla – NT	Skage	1908
Jens Eliasen	Vining, MN	Kolvereid – NT	Aarfor	1893
Miss Laura Eng	Northwood, ND	Namdalen – NT		1893
Ole Engen	Fergus Falls, MN	Holtaalen – ST		1867
Peter Enokson	Fergus Falls, MN	Frosta - NT	Aanan	1893
Ole E. Estvold	Fergus Falls, MN	Verdalsørem – NT	Østvold	1880
Jens Fossen	Fergus Falls, MN	Stjørdalen – NT	Almo	1865
Michael J. Fossen	Fergus Falls, MN	Stjørdalen – NT		*1865
Ole J. Fossen	Fergus Falls, MN	Stjørdalen – NT		1865
Gunder Frigaard	Cooperstown, ND	Stjørdalen – NT		1866
Otto Furreness	Underwood, MN	Namdalen – NT	Furrenæset	1887
John Furuness	Fergus Falls, MN	Opdal - ST	Furunes	1898
Albert Gjerset	Fergus Falls, MN	Frænen, f. 1874	Eidem	*1871
Magnus Gjerset	Watson, MN	Frænen – MoR	Eidem	1871
Oluf Gjerset	Montevideo, MN	Frænen- MoR	Eidem	1871
O. [Ole] A. Grande	Fergus Falls, MN	Ørlandet - ST	Grande	1893
Christian Haarsager	Litchville, ND	Father from Strinda		*1880
Elias Haarsager	Grisvold, ND	Stadsbygden - ST		1880
John P. Haave	Fergus Falls, MN	Stjørdalen – NT	Haave	1867
John P. Haave, Jr.	Fergus Falls, MN	Stjørdalen – NT		1888
Edw. Haldorsen	Rothsay, MN	Stod – NT		*1865

* *Charter member born in America. The year represents when their first family member emigrated.*

Charter Members of Trønderlaget of America 1908-09

Name	1908 Residence	Home area	Farm name	Emig.
Martin O. Hall	Fergus Falls, MN	Veblungsnes -MoR		1872
Jonas O. Hallan	Fergus Falls	Levangerskogn – NT		*1865
S.O. Hammer	Pelican Rapids, MN	Inderøy - NT	Hoe	1869
J. O. Hatling	Dalton, MN	Stod – NT		1865
J. Hatlinghus	Fergus Falls, MN	Stod/Steinkjer-NT		1907
O.C. Hauan	Mayville, ND	Overhalla - NT		1866
Bernt B. Haugan	Fergus Falls, MN	Ekne, Skogn – NT		1872
O.B. Haugan	Fergus Falls, MN	Ekne, Skogn – NT		1872
John Hindrum	Fergus Falls, MN	Leksvikstrand – NT		1869
John Hogstad	Moorhead, MN	Inderøy – NT	Hogstad	1883
Arnt O. Huseby	Fergus Falls, MN	Stjørdalen (far)	Huseby	*1869
Severin Huseby	Fergus Falls, MN	Stjørdalen – NT	Vestre Husby	1881
Ulrick Huus	Fergus Falls, MN	Frøya –ST	Dyrø	1891
Endre Ingebregtsen	Brandon, MN	Stjørdalen – NT	Leren	1866
Jacob Jensen	Fergus Falls, MN	Frøya – ST	Gjessingen	1907
Paul Johanson	Fergus Falls, MN	Inderøy – NT	Watten	1883
Fred Johnsen	Fergus Falls, MN	Bolsøy - MoR	Aarønes	1890
Chris Johnson	Fergus Falls, MN	Steinkjer – NT		1867
Martin Johnson	Fergus Falls, MN	Verdalen – NT	Storvukku	1882
Theo Johnson	Fergus Falls, MN	Verdalen – NT	Lerfald	1870
Anton Jordahl	Fergus Falls, MN	Trondheim – ST		1888
Mrs. Jordahl	Fergus Falls, MN	Trondheim – ST		1892
Johan Knudsen	Wendell, MN	Orkedalen - ST	Kvamsbakken	1882
Eilert Koefod	Glenwood, MN	Kristiansund-MoR		1881
Mariane Lein	Fergus Falls, MN	Verdalen – NT	Haga	1883
Peter Lein	Fergus Falls, MN	Skogn – NT	Lein	1880
O.O. Lerfald	Fergus Falls, MN	Verdalen – NT		1866
S. O. Leirfallom	Mohall, ND	Stjørdalen – NT	Søndre Leirfall	1889
Jon Lervik	Morris, MN	Stjørdalen – NT	Aas	
Peter A. Loktu	Fergus Falls, MN	Frosta – NT		1893
Mrs. Odin Løseth	Underwood, MN	Namdalen – NT		1901
Edvard Lund	Vining, MN	Kolvereid – NT	Lund	1889
J. [John] Lyng	Dalton, MN	Verdalen – NT	Lyngmellem	1902
Emil Middelfart	Fargo, ND	Trondheim – ST		1906
Stasius Nordgaard	Rothsay, MN	Stod - NT	Norgaard	1867

* *Charter member born in America. The year represents when their first family member emigrated.*

CHARTER MEMBERS

Charter Members of Trønderlaget of America 1908-09

Name	1908 Residence	Home area	Farm name	Emig.
Ole Nygaard	Fergus Falls, MN	Orkedalen - ST		1870
Mads Olson	Milnor, ND	Stjørdalen/Hegra - NT		1880
Olaus Olson	Grisvold, ND	Frosta - NT		1880
Oluf E. Orstad	Fergus Falls, MN	Verdalen - NT	Aarstad	1884
Lars O. Overmoen	Warren, ND	Verdalen - NT	Overmoen	1870
Gjertru Pedersdatter	Milnor, ND	Hegra - NT		1880
Christ Pederson	Minneapolis, MN	Stjørdalen - NT	Ydstiness	1887
Nils Pederson	Fergus Falls, MN	Levanger – NT	Grevskot	1886
Erik Peterson	Galchutt, ND	Rennebu – ST	Haarstad	1888
Cornelius Petterson	Fergus Falls	Karlsøy - Troms		
Ingolf Petterson	Morris, MN	Trondheim – ST	Steinkjer/Welde	1875
Martin Rathe	Fergus Falls, MN	Trondheim – ST	Strinden/Rathe	1881
Ditlef G. Ristad	Fergus Falls, MN	Overhalla – NT	Ristad	1887
B. Rønning	Milnor, ND	Horrig – ST	Rønningen	1880
Martin Rosvold	Fergus Falls, MN	Verdalen – NT		1869
Jon Røst	Ulen, MN	Leksviken – NT	Røstad	1888
Mrs. O. A. Rustad	Dalton, MN	Steinkjer/Sparbu–NT	Søndre Gade	1866
Johannes P. Schei	Dalton, MN	Verdalen – NT	Schei	1867
Ole J. Schei	Fergus Falls, MN	Verdalen – NT		*1867
Haakon Selness	Vining, MN	Verdalen – NT		1903
Theo O. Sjørdal	Underwood, MN	Verdalen – NT		1871
Iver O. Skistad	Elizabet, MN	Overhalla – NT	Skistad	1866
S. M. Skrove	Dalton, MN	Verdalen – NT	Skrove	1882
Oline (Dahl) Skrove	Dalton, MN	Steinkjer – NT	f. i Amerika	*1866
O. S. Sneve	Brookings, SD	Opdal – ST	Sneve	1871
Olaf A. Solberg	Fergus Falls, MN	Verdalen f. 1872		*1867
A. [Anfinn] Solem	Fergus Falls, MN	Strinden – ST	Fredriksted	1879
C.P. Stav	Aastad, MN	Strinden – ST		1870
B.M. Stene	Underwood, MN	Verdalen – NT		1893
Isak Strinden	Ottertail Co, MN	Stod – NT	Strinden	1866
Anton Sumstad	Ashby, MN	Bjørnør – ST		1898
Thorolf Svensgaard	Erhard, MN	Kristiansund–MoR		1882
N. O. Svorkmo	Fergus Falls, MN	Orkedalen – ST		1891
A. B. Thompson	Henning, MN	Selbu – ST	Evjen	*1867
John Thompson	Brandon, MN	Stjørdalen – NT		1865

* *Charter member born in America. The year represents when their first family member emigrated.*

Charter Members of Trønderlaget of America 1908-09

Name	1908 Residence	Home area	Farm name	Emig.
John B. Thompson	Battle Lake, MN	Selbu – ST	Evjen	*1867
Nels B. Thompson	Fergus Falls, MN	Selbu – ST	Evjen	*1867
Benjamin Trøen	Glenwood, MN	Stod – NT	Storvestre	1871
Mrs. A.A. Trovaten	Fargo, ND	Stjørdalen – NT	Lillemoe	1866
Rev J. O. Wangberg	Mohall, ND	Frosta – NT		1892
Dr. Jorgen Vigen	Fergus Falls, MN	Selbu – ST	Vigen	1869
Iver M. Wick	Dalton, MN	Beitstaden – NT	Vik	1869
Ove Wick	Fergus Falls, MN	Beitstaden – NT	Vik	1866
T.C. Wigen	Elizabet, MN	Frosta – NT		1869
Gunder Winkjer	Garfield, MN	Levanger – NT	Vinkjær	1864
Johannes B. Wist	Decorah, IA	Sparbu/Inderøy-NT	Sund	1887
Einar Wold	Galchutt, ND	Rennebu – ST	Wold	1876
Casper T. Wollan	Glenwood, MN	Stod – NT	Wollan	1860
Michal A. Wollan	Glenwood, MN	Stod – NT	Wollan	1860
T.C. Wollan	Fergus Falls, MN	Stod – NT	Wollan	1866

* *Charter member born in America. The year represents when their first family member emigrated.*

Nidaros Domkirke, Trondheim

CHARTER MEMBERS

Trønderlag of America Charter Members

The following people are recognized as Charter Members of the Trønderlag of America. They joined the organization from 1908-1909. More detailed biographies of all Trønderlag Charter members will be included in the *Trønderlag Aarbok 2008*, available in late 2008. Information on ordering *Aarbok 2008* is found at the end of this book.

For a variety of reasons, many Norwegians changed their surnames when they immigrated. The names that appear here are the way the Charter Members "signed in" when they joined *Trønderlaget*. We suspect that the names were handwritten or verbally provided and later transcribed so changes and errors may have occurred in that process. Names that we found to be regularly used by the member but which were different from the "official Trønderlag name" are written in the following short biographies as /aka. In parenthesis we have placed the name as they may have been known in Norway – with the patronymic and farm name.

Information about the Charter Members was obtained through research in both U.S. and Norwegian records as well as through information provided by descendants of the Charter Members. We tried to confirm all information with official records.

Aalberg, Martin (Lornts Martin Andersen Aalberg), b. July 1859 Sparbu, Nord-Trøndelag, Norway; d. 3 Oct. 1823 Hennepin Co., MN. Parents: Anders Petersen Aalberg (b. 1825 Sparbu) & Hannah Hansdatter

Most charter members, like other emigrants from Trøndelag, left Norway by departing from Trondheim. Above is the shipping office of the Cunard Line in Trondheim in the late 1800s. Photo used with permission of Borge Solem.

65

(b. 1827 Inderøien). Family residing on Haugen (Plads) farm in Sparbu in 1865. Martin emigrated from Sparbu to Minneapolis 4 May 1881. Left Trondheim on feeder ship *Tasso*. Settled first in Minneapolis, then in Henning, Otter Tail Co., MN in 1892. Married 8 Nov. 1884 to Trina Quam (1864-1925) who emigrated from Norway in 1883. Occupation: Civil engineer; county surveyor. Children: Arthur, Harry, Florence, Leonard, and Lily Aalberg.

Aasnes, C. L. /aka Cornelius Aasness (Cornelius Larsen Åsnes), b. 18 May 1831 Nandalseidet/ Beitstaden, Nord-Trøndelag, Norway; d. 28 May 1915, Fergus Falls, Otter Tail Co., MN. Parents: Lars Kjelsen Åsnes (1801-1862) & Elen Olsdotter Åsnes (b. 1801 Namdalseid). Emigrated in 1864. Settled first in Decorah, Iowa (1864-1868), then in Otter Tail Co., MN. Brother Edward L. Aasnes emigrated in 1866 and also settled in Otter Tail Co. Married Malena Mikkelsdtr. Støstad (b. Kvam, Norway) on 25 April 1867 in Decorah, IA. Occupation: Farmer. Cornelius and daughter Mary took a trip to Norway in 1895. Children: Louise, Ole, Edward, Christian, and Marie/Mary Aasnes.

Cornelius L. Aasnes (1831-1915)

Aune, Ingebrigt H. (Ingebrigt Hanssen), b. 1863 Melhus, Sør-Trøndelag, Norway; d. 19 June 1930 Fergus Falls, MN. Parents: Hans Johnsen (b. 1928 Buviken) & Randi Ingebrigtsdatter (b. 1840 Melhus). Family was living on Onsøitrøen farm in Byneset in 1865. Emigrated 3 May 1882 from Trondheim to Rothsay, MN, departing on the feeder ship *Tasso*. Settled in Fergus Falls, MN. Occupation: Stone mason, butcher at Fergus Packing Plant 1910-1930. Unmarried. No children.

Baglo, Nicolai (Nikolai Kristiansen Baglo), b. 26 Sep 1871 Værdalen, Nord-Trøndelag; d. 1963 Cumberland, WI. Parents: Kristian Nikolaisen (b. 1848 Værdalen) & Anne Arentsdtr. Bergsvald (b. 1848 Støren). Living on Baglovald Baglo farm in Verdal in 1875. Emigrated with his family 30 Aug 1886 from

CHARTER MEMBERS

Værdalen to Fergus Falls, MN, leaving on the ship *Thingvalla* via Christiania. Settled in Fergus Falls & later Lakeland, Barron Co., WI. Married about 1896 to Louisa Hedman (1878-1948). Occupation: Wheat buyer, flour mill laborer, Wisconsin dairy. Children: Evelyn, Blanch, Burton, Clarence, Mildred, Francis, Robert, Marion, and Carl Baglo.

Bye, Carl P. (Carl Peter Pedersen), b. 12 Nov. 1857 Værdalen, Nord-Trøndelag; d. 5 Nov. 1926 Fergus Falls, MN. Parents: Peder Hanssen Byvaldet (b. 1803 Holtålen) & Marit Andersdatter (b. 1813 Støren). Family living on Storøen farm in Verdal in 1865. Emigrated 1 April 1880 from Værdalen to Toronto, Canada. Settled in Sargeant Co., ND, then Fergus Falls, MN. Occupation: Harvester Company in Argentina South America; later a nurse at Fergus Falls State Hospital. No children.

Nicolai & Louisa Baglo

Bye, Hans P. (Hans Peter Martinussen Bye), b. 21 Sept. 1875 Værdalen, Nord-Trøndelag, Norway; d. 31 Oct. 1946 Otter Tail Co., MN. Parents: Martinus Eliassen Maritvoldvald (b. 1847) & Oleanna Johannesdtr.(b. 1839). Emigrated 5 April 1882 from Værdalen to Fergus Falls, MN with his mother and siblings, leaving on the feedership *Tasso* to Englund. Settled in Fergus Falls. He and his sisters moved to Duluth in 1890s where Hans worked as a driver for a meat store business owned by one of his sister's future in-laws. Married Marie Stangvik on 22 April 1900 and moved back to Fergus Falls. Occupation: Worked in flour mills, grocery business with his brother John M. Bye, also was Alderman for the 4th Ward Fergus Falls. One foster child, Margaret.

Bye, John E. (Johannes Eliasen Bye), b. 5 June 1866 Værdalen, Nord-Trøndelag; d.

From Left: Johannes E. Bye, son Eivind, wife Anne Ness, daughter-in-law Pearl holding granddaughter Diane and Eivind, Jr. on tricycle.

67

11 Nov. 1940 Fergus Falls, MN. Parents: Elias Eliason Byvald (b. 1820 Verdal) & Gurianna Hansdtr. (b. 1821 Verdal). Emigrated abt. 1886-87. Settled in Fergus Falls, MN. Married Anne Ness on 22 Dec. 1891. Occupation: Worked in flour mills. Child: Eivind George Bye, b. 1897.

Bye, John M. (Johan Edvard Martinussen Bye), b. 28 Dec. 1869 Værdalen, Nord-Trøndelag; d. 1 June 1922 Fergus Falls, MN. Parents: Martinius Elias Maritvoldvald (b. 1847) & Oleanna Johansdtr. (b. 1839). Emigrated 5 April 1882 from Værdalen to Fergus Falls, MN with his mother and siblings. Settled in Fergus Falls. Married Gertrude Hagen. Occupation: Worked in grocery business with his brother (H. P. Bye & Co.). Children: Mabel, George, John, Myrtle, and Margaret Bye.

The children of Martin Bye: charter member Hans Peter (left), Marie, Anna and charter member John M. Bye (right).

Dahl, B. C. (Børre Christofersen Haarstad), b. 24 Oct. 1830 Østre Gausdal, Oppland; d. 1 Nov. 1908 Otter Tail Co, MN. Parents: Christopher Olsen & Marit Johannesdatter. Emigrated with his brothers Ole and Simon in Spring 1865 or 1866 from Beitstad, Nord-Trøndelag - first to Iowa, then to Otter Tail Co., MN. Married 8 Feb. 1858 in Beitstad to Anna Helena Michaelsdatter Utulvika (Wick), b. 26 Jan. 1836 Beitstad. Occupation: Farmer in Tumuli Twp., Otter Tail Co., MN. Children: Olena (Oline) Margaret and Kaia Dahl. Daughter Olena married Trønder Sigurd Skrove in 1893; both were Charter Members.

Dahl, Gunder (Gunder Olesen Dahl), b. 19 April 1845 Gausdal, Oppland; d. 16 Feb. 1923 Fergus Falls, MN. Parents: Ole Christophersen Dahl (b. 1817) & Oline Gundersdatter Olstad (b. 1816). Living at Søndre Gade in Sparbu, NT in 1865. Emigrated from Bergen to Quebec 6 April 1866 with his mother and six younger siblings. Settled in Rochester, MN until 1869, then

CHARTER MEMBERS

Alexandria and finally Fergus Falls in 1874. Married 6 Feb. 1875 to Anna M. Thompson (b. 1855 MN). Occupation: Painter, merchant, county commissioner. Children: Henry G. and three who died in infancy. The father, Ole Dahl, coming to America with his brothers Simon and Børre, homesteaded land where Dalton, MN now stands. The village was named for him. Gunder's sister Randine married O. M. Wick, sister Caroline married G. O. Hammer and sister Anne Othelie married Oliver Rustad.

Gunder O. Dahl (1845-1923)

Dorrum, I. (Ingebrigt Ingebrigtsen Dørrum), b. 27 Dec 1878 Opdal, Sør-Trøndelag; d. 6 Jan. 1952 Decorah, IA. Parents: Ingebrigt R. Dørrum & Marit Olsdatter. His father was a farmer and postal clerk. Emigrated 15 March 1899 from Trondheim to Seattle, WA. After moving around to further his education at Pacific Lutheran Academy, Parkland, WA and Luther College, settled in Fergus Falls and Decorah, IA. Married in 1912 to Anna Christiansen (b. 1879) of Boston, MA. Occupation: College professor. Taught Norwegian at Luther College 1923-retirement in 1949. Secretary-treasurer of Trønderlaget from 1912-1919 and Aarbok editor. Children: Eleanor V. and Solveig D. Dorrum.

Ecker, Ole (Ole Williamsen Ekker), b. 1 Dec. 1861 at Skage in Overhalla, Nord-Trøndelag; d. 29 Sept. 1941 St. Louis Co., MN. Parents: William Johansen Ekker (b. 1831 Grongs) & Hanna Christine Pedersdatter (b. 1838 Beitstad). Family living on Skage farm in Overhalla in 1865. Emigrated in 22 March 1882 from Namsos to Hudson, WI. Settled in Cloquet, MN and later Duluth. Married Carrie Opdahl about 1890. Occupation: House painter. Children: Perry, William, John, Anna L., Hannah E., Peter, and Olympia Ecker.

Ole (1861-1941) and Karen Ecker from Overhalla, Nord-Trøndelag

69

Eidem, Ole (Ole Aslaksen Eidem), b. 27 Aug. 1853 Fræna, More og Romsdal; d. 2 Oct. 1910 Chippewa Co., MN. Parents: Aslak Ellingsen and Karn Maria Olsdatter (b. 1834 Fraenens). Residing on Eidem farm in Fræna in 1865. Half brother to Albert Gjerset. Emigrated 1871 with his mother, step-father and siblings. Settled in Watson, MN. Married abt 1879 to Stella Gumm of Benson. Occupation: General store keeper. No children.

Einan, O. P. /aka Ole Paulson (Ole Paulson Einan), b. 21 Oct. 1858 Selbu, Sør-Trøndelag; d. 26 March 1942 in Hennepin Co., MN. Parents: Paul Olsen (b. 1826 Selbu) & Brynhild Thomasdatter (b. 1826 Selbu). Living on farm Berge Enan in Selbu in 1865 and 1875. In 1900 the farm was called Einan. Emigrated 28 March 1900 from Selbu to Elk Point, SD. Settled in Brule, SD, then Carlisle, MN. Married 9 April 1883 in Norway to Johanna Haldorsdatter Borseth (b. 1 Sept. 1861, d. 17 April 1937). Wife and children emigrated 13 June 1907 to Carlisle. Occupation: Farmer, laborer in factory. Children: Brynhild, Marit, Gjertrud, Paul, Pauline, Paul Teodor, Olaf Selmer, Johan Martin, Olga Johanna, Johan Magne Einan.

Ole Paulson & Johanna Einan

Ekker, Per /aka Perry Ecker (Per Johannesen Ekker), b. 1 April 1887 Namdalen, Overhalla, Nord-Trøndelag; d. 14 March 1958 Fargo, ND. Nephew to Ole Ecker. Parents: Johannes Williamsen Ekker (b. 1855 Overhalla, Skage; d. 1896 Skage) & Marie Andreasdatter (b. 1858 Overhalla; d. after 1908 U.S.). Family residing on Skage farm in Overhalla in 1875. Emigrated 27 May 1908 to Fergus Falls, MN. Settled in Otter Tail Co. Married 21 March 1925

Perry Ecker from Overhalla, about 1910

CHARTER MEMBERS

in Fergus Falls to Alice Nelson (b. 14 April 1898; d. 2 Dec 1960). Occupation: Laborer, farmer. Served in WWI. Children: Dorothy, Elizabeth, Marlene, Ellen, James, Phillip, and Kenneth Ecker.

Eliasen, Jens (Jens Johannes Eliasen), b. 22 July 1838 Fosnes, Nord-Trøndelag; d. 24 Aug. 1918 Otter Tail Co., MN. Parents: Elias Andersen Kvernvik (1812-1864) & Berthe Serine Rasmusdatter Birkeväg. Emigrated 15 March 1893 from Foldereid to Winnipeg, Manitoba. Settled in Nidaros Twp, Otter Tail Co., MN. Married Lotte K. Olsdatter (b. abt 1845) d. 5 Feb. 1928) before 1865 in Norway. Occupation: Laborer. Children: Petra Bergitte, Elise Margrethe, Hanna Ovidia, Lina Julie, Anton Ovid, and Konrad Julius Eliasen.

Eng, Miss Laura (Laura Aletta Eriksdatter Eidshaug), b. 16 May 1870 Kolvereid, Nord Trøndelag; d. 26 Jan. 1956 Hennepin Co., MN. Parents: Erik Christiansen Eidshaug/Nubedal (b. 1823 Kolvereid, d. 1910 WI) & Marianne Fredrikke Larsdatter Bjørge (b. 1828 Vikna, d. 1912 U.S.). Emigrated 2 August 1893 from Trondheim to Boston, landing in Detroit, MI 24 Aug. 1893. Settled in Eau Claire, WI, Hillsboro, ND, Minneapolis and St. Paul, MN. Occupation: Trained nurse. Children: None.

Engen, Ole (Ole Eriksen Engan), b. 5 Aug. 1849 Aalen, Haltdalen, Sør-Trøndelag; d. 30 June 1914 Fergus Falls, MN. Died from a runaway horse accident in Fergus Falls. Parents: Erik Johnsen Engan (1793-1882) & Ingeborg Pedersdatter Flatberg (1805-1893 Haltdalen). Emigrated 30 April 1867 from Aalen to Quebeck with brother Peder and sister Guri. Settled in Winnesheck Co., IA, then to Minnesota – in Otter Tail Co. before 1900. Married 30 May 1891 in Fergus Falls to

Ole Engen children: John Edward, Ingeborg Belle, Ingvold Oliver, Albert Richard, Joseph (Joe) Alexander, and Sylvia Marie.

71

Inga Marie Arneson (1869-1955). Occupation: Farmer. Children: John Edward, Belle Emily, Agnes, Ingvald Oliver, Arthur M., Albert Richard, Joseph Alexander, Sylvia, and James A. Engen.

Enokson, Peter (Peder Magnus Enochsen), b. 17 Sept. 1877 Frosta, Nord-Trøndelag; d. 1 Dec. 1968 Otter Tail Co., MN. Parents: Enoch Peterson (b. abt 1849) & Mattie Peterson (abt 1837-1935). Emigrated abt 1893 with his mother. Settled in Fergus Falls, MN. Married 1 Jan. 1914 to Telle Nicoline (b. 1879 Baldwin, WI; d. 1957 Henning, MN). Occupation: Plasterer, brick mason. No children.

Estvold, Ole S. (Olaus Sevaldsen Østvoldvaldet), b. 20 Oct. 1854 Verdal, Nord-Trøndelag; d. 30 Nov. 1921 Otter Tail Co., MN. Parents: Sevald Olsen (b. 1813 Verdal) & Ingeborganna Jensdatter (b. 1816 Inderøien). In 1865 the family was living on the Østvoldvald Finden farm in Verdal. Ole emigrated 14 April 1880 from Værdalen with a destination of Melrose, MN. His occupation at the time was listed as tailor. Settled in Otter Tail Co., MN – first in Fergus Falls, then in Aarstad Twp. Married in 1882 to Marie Larsdatter Vistavald (1853-1937) who emigrated 13 April 1882 from Værdalen to Fergus Falls at the age of 28 at Ole's request. Occupation: Farmer. Children: Ole Marius, Lewis S., Arthur B., Inga Christine, Emil O., Martin, Oscar and one child who died young.

Olaus Estvold (1854-1921)

Fossen, Jens O. (Jens Olsen Fossen), b. 6 Oct. 1833 Geilhaugen under Almo in Hegra, Nord-Trøndelag; d. 22 June 1919 Fergus Falls, MN. Parents: Ola Jensen Brende (1768-1838) & Marit Olsdatter Gederås (1795-1879). Emigrated with his wife and family 4 May 1865 from Trondheim aboard the bark *Bergen*. During the 14 week journey, two of their children died. Settled 1865-1870 in Goodhue Co., MN, then 1870 Fergus Falls. Married 11 April

Jens and Kristine Fossen from Hegra

1859 in Norway to Kristine Larsdatter Rømo (15 Sept. 1830-22 June 1919). Jens and his wife Kristine were killed in a cyclone that hit Otter Tail County, MN in June 1919. Occupation: Farmer. Children: Ole, Louise, John, Gurine, and Michael Fossen.

Fossen, Michael J., b. 13 April 1874 Dane Prairie, Otter Tail Co., MN; d. 30 April 1920 Fergus Falls, MN. Parents: Jens Olsen Fossen (1833 Hegra, Nord-Trøndelag-1919 Fergus Falls) & Kristine Larsdatter Rømo (1830-1919). No emigration. Lived in Fergus Falls, MN. Married 18 June 1897 to Tonetta Boen (1872-1962), sister of Congressman H. E. Boen. Occupation: Grocer. Was also a charter member of Sons of Norway Heimskringla Lodge in Fergus Falls. Children: Klara, Ida, Julian, Edwin, and Mabel Fossen.

Michael J. Fossen (1874-1920)

Fossen, Ole J. (Ola Jensen Fossen), b. 17 July 1859 Dalsaunskogen, Hegra, Nord-Trøndelag; d. 8 Jan. 1945, Fergus Falls, MN. Parents: Jens Olsen Fossen (1833 Hegra, Nord Trøndelag-1919 Fergus Falls) & Kristine Larsdatter Rømo (1830-1919). Emigrated in 1865 from Trondheim with his family. Settled 1865-1870 in Goodhue Co., MN, from 1870 in Fergus Falls. Married 16 Oct. 1884 to Olive Olson Satre (16 Aug. 1859-16 May 1937). Occupation: Owned a roller feed mill; later operated a feed and seed store. Charter member and first president of Sons of Norway Heimskringla Lodge in Fergus Falls. Children: George, Theodore, and Henry Fossen.

Ole J. Fossen (1859-1945) from Hegra, brother of Michael Fossen

Frigaard, Gunder (Gunder Christophersen Frigaard), b. 24 July 1864 Stjørdalen, Nord-Trøndelag; d. 9 Nov. 1929 Bottineau, Griggs Co., ND. Parents: Kristoffer Andersen Frigård (b. 1823 Øvre Størdalen) & Mali Gunnarsdtr. Klefsåslien (b. 1826 Øvre Størdalen). Family was living at Fossum vestre farm in Hegra in 1865. Emigrated at age one in 1866 with his family and arrived in Quebec 9 June 1866 on board the bark *Neptunus*. Settled first

Gunder and Marie Frigaard with their twelve children in Bottineau, North Dakota.

in Zumbrota, MN; 1903 to Cooperstown, ND. Attended St. Olaf College, then taught school in Goodhue and Lac Qui Parle counties. Married 7 March 1891 to Marie Vingness (1870-1929) of Zumbrota, MN. Occupation: 1906-1922 Clerk of District Court at Cooperstown, ND. Children: Martin, George, Harold, Adolph, Myrtle, Thelma, Marie, Arthur, Bertha, Agnes, Clara, and Gertrude Frigaard.

Furreness, Otto (Otto Alexandersen Furrunæs), b. 27 March 1964 Overhalla, Nord-Trøndelag; d. 3 June 1933 Otter Tail Co., MN. Parents: Alexander Sellæg (b. 1832 Overhalla) & Daarethe Olsdatter (b. 1837 Overhalla). Emigrated 9 March 1887 from Trondheim under the name of Otto A. Seleg, age 22, to Thomson, MN. Settled first in Thompson, MN then to Otter Tail Co., MN about 1890. Otto returned to Norway about 1898 and married widow Marie Andreasdatter (Hammer) Ecker (b. 1858 Overhalla). Marie had five children with her first husband, Johannes Ekker. Otto A. Furrunæs emigrated with his new family 16 Sept. 1901 to Underwood, MN. Occupation: Farmer. Children with Marie: Johannes and Dagny.

John Furuness (1871-1925)

Furuness, John (Johan Olsen Furrunæs), b. 20 June 1871 Opdal, Sør-Trøndelag; d. 10 Aug. 1925 Finley, Steele Co., ND. Parents: Ole Jonsen Furrunæs (d. before 1875) & Marit Nilsdatter Furunes (b. 1836 Sundals sogn). Emigrated 30 March 1898 from Trondheim to Chicago, IL. Settled in Fergus Falls 1898-1912, then Finley, ND 1912-1925. Married Bessie A. Myhra (b. 1881-1965) after 1910. Occupation: Watchmaker and jeweler – owned his own store in North Dakota. Children: Oscar and Kenneth Furuness.

Gjerset (Gjerseth), Albert, b. 23 Aug. 1874 Big Bend, Chippewa Co, MN; d. 13 Feb. 1931 Minneapolis, MN. Parents: Ole S. Gjerset (b. 1827 Gryttens) & Karen Marie Eidem (b. 1822 Frænens) living on Eidem farm in Frænen, Møre og Romsdal in 1865. No emigration. Parents emigrated in 1871. Lived in Tunsberg (1900), Fergus Falls (1910) and Minneapolis, MN (1925-1931). Married in 1897 to Anne Johnson (b. 1877). Occupation: Store clerk, life insurance agent. Children: Kenneth O., Esther Karen, Ezra Mozart, Oswald Seymour, Ruth V., Elzabad (son), Ava B., Anna Mona, and Russell Carolus Gjerset.

Albert O. Gjerset (1874-1931)

Gjerset (Gjerseth), Magnus (Magnus Olsen Gjerset/Eidem), b. 6 Sept. 1868 Eidem farm, Frænen, Møre og Romsdal; d. 3 Feb. 1951 Chippewa Co., MN. Parents: Ole S. Gjerset (b. 1827 Gryttens) & Karen Marie Eidem (b. 1822 Frænens) living on Eidem farm in Frænen, Møre og Romsdal in 1865. Emigrated with his parents and siblings in 1871. Settled in Big Bend, Chippewa Co., MN. Married about 1900 to 1) Sarah Aamot (b. 1874 Norway, d. 1911/12); 2) Frances Gomol (b. 1862 Germany). Occupation: Farmer in Big Bend on the Gjerset family farm. Magnus was a brother to charter members Albert & Oluf Gjerset and Caroline who married charter member Thomas C. Wollan. His brother, Prof. Knut Gjerset of Luther College in Decorah, joined Trønderlaget in 1910. He was also half brother to charter member Ole Eidem. Children with Sarah: Oscar F. and Ethel Gjerset. Children with Frances: Walter Magnus Gjerset.

Gjerset (Gjerseth), Oluf (Oluf Olsen Gjerset/Eidem), b. 1 June 1858 Møre og Romsdal; d. 29 May 1941 Montevideo, MN. Parents: Ole S. Gjerset (b. 1827 Gryttens) & Karen Marie Eidem (b. 1822 Frænens) living on Eidem farm in Frænen, Møre og Romsdal in 1865. Emigrated with his parents and siblings in 1871, departing from Bergen to Hull. Settled in Montevideo, MN. Single, no children. Oluf was a brother to charter members Albert & Magnus Gjerset and Caroline who married charter member Thomas C. Wollan. His brother, Knut Gjerset, was a professor at Luther College in Decorah. Occupation: Attorney, Minnesota State Senator, county attorney, city attorney for Montevideo.

Grande, O. [Ole] A. (Ole Andersen Grande), b. 18 Oct. 1871 Ørlandet, Sør-Trøndelag; d. 26 Dec. 1951 Burbank, Los Angeles Co., CA. Parents: Anders Christiansen Grande (b. 1829 Ørlandet) & Oline Brodersdatter (b. 1838 Skjørn). Emigrated 15 Feb. 1893 from Trondheim to La Crosse, WI on the feeder ship *Volo* to Hull, England and from there by train to Liverpool, then on the *S/S Numidian* which arrived at the Port of Halifax 5 March 1893. Settled first in La Crosse, then in 1896 Fergus Falls, MN. Married in 1905 to Elizabeth Shellman (1875-1963). Occupation: Carpenter, foreman in a manufacturing plant, building contractor. Children: Harold Shellman, John Frederick, Elizabeth Inger Day (adopted niece), and Beatrice Ann Grande.

Ole and Elizabeth Grande with two grandchildren

Haarsager, Christian /aka Christian Norman Horsager, b. 10 July 1882 Pelican Rapids, MN; d. March 1971 Tacoma, Pierce, WA. Parents: Johan Nielsen Haarsager (b. 1852 Stadsbygd, Sør-Trøndelag) & Martha (b. 1837 Norway). In 1900 the parents had been married 18 years, probably a second marriage for Martha. The father emigrated 26 May 1880 from Stadsbygden to Breckenridge, MN, leaving Trondheim on the Dampskib *Tasso*. Christ married Ellen. b. 11 Sept. 1881 Norway; d. Jan. 1974 Litchfield, ND. Ellen had emigrated in 1903. Occupation: Farmer. One adopted child: Birger Norman (Ronning) Horsager, b. 3 May 1911.

CHARTER MEMBERS

Haarsager, Elias (Elias Jensen Haarsager), b. 23 March 1855 Stadsbygd, Sør-Trøndelag; d. 28 Sept. 1926 Litchville, ND. A twin to Johan Jenssen Haarsager who remained in Norway and became a teacher. Parents: Jens Jenssen Haarsager (b. 1806 Stadsbygden) & Olava Eriksdatter Pukstad (b. 1817 Stadsbygden). Emigrated 26 May 1880 from Stadsbygden with destination of Breckinridge, MN. Settled a short time in Rothsay, MN, then Litchville, ND. Married 17 May 1884 in La Moure Co., ND to Kjersten Johanne Pedersdatter Fenstad (b. 2 Jan. 1868 Stadsbygd). Occupation: Farmer. 16 children: Olga, Inga Amanda, Jennie, Peder Edwin, Jens Oliver, Clara Elida, Julia, Dagne Constance, Conrad Adolph, William Joseph, Ella Charlotte, Cora Alette, Gene Josephine, Ralph Oliver, Clifford John, and Hazel Audrey Lucille Haarsager.

Haave, John P. (Johan Pedersen Haave), b. 14 Jan. 1839 Nedre Stjørdalen; d. 10 Oct. 1926 Fergus Falls, MN. Parents: Peter Johnsen Haave (b. 1809) & Sollaug Johnsdatter Størfløren (b. 1814). Emigration with his wife: 30 April 1867 from Størdalen to Quebec leaving on the ship *Neptunus*; arrived in Quebec 19 June 1867. Settled first in Red Wing (1867), then in Fergus Falls, MN (from 1871). Mr. & Mrs. Haave started for Fergus Falls to look for land to homestead with two other families: Mr. & Mrs. Ole Huseby (parents of charter member Arnt Huseby) and Mr. & Mrs. T. Bjorgum. Married Martha Johnsdatter Ertsgaard (1840-1922) on 12 April 1867 in Stjørdalen, Norway. Occupation: Grocery business from 1884; also Otter Tail County Commissioner (1896-1900), Trustee of Park Region Lutheran College, and various municipal and local offices. No children.

John P. Haave (1839-1926)
Photo from Otter Tail County Historical Museum

John P. Haave, Jr. (Johan P. Haave), b. 15 April 1876 Trondheim; d. 5 May 1935 Fergus Falls, MN. Parents: Peder Pedersen Haave

(1845-1922) & Ellen (1846-1900). Nephew of charter member John P. Haave who he lived with from age 12. Emigrated 5 Sept. 1888 from N. Størdalen to Minneapolis, MN, leaving on the *Hero*. Settled in Fergus Falls, MN. Married 5 Jan. 1910 to Clara Nelson (1878-1966). Occupation: Grocery clerk (1900), Deputy Treasurer of Otter Tail County (1911). Children: Edna C., Helen L., Mildred Elizabeth Haave.

Haldorson, Edw. (Edward Haldorsen), b. 17 Dec. 1872 in Oscar Twp, Otter Tail Co., MN; d. 3 Sept. 1959 Otter Tail Co., MN. Parents: Mikkel Haldorsen (1820-1909) & Ellen Mortine Christophersdotter Strendau (1827-1911). Parents emigrated about 1865 from Stod, Nord-Trøndelag and settled in Otter Tail Co., MN. Married Lena Toso Pederson (b. 1888) in Otter Tail Co. 17 Dec. 1943. Occupation: Farmer. Seven step-children.

Hall, Martin O. (Morten Olsen), b. 1 Feb. 1843 Grytens, Romsdalen; d. 29 April 1920 Fergus Falls, MN. Parents: Ole Larssen (b. 1798 Gausdal, Oppland) & Mari Paulsdatter (b. 1819 Vaage, Nordland). Emigrated about 1871/72. In the Trønderlag records his home area is listed as Veblungsnes. Settled in Calumet, MI (1880), Minnesota (1884), Hall, Sargent, ND (1880s-1904), Fergus Falls (1904-1912), Minneapolis (1912-1919), Fergus Falls (1919-1920). Married abt 1886 to Gina J. (b. Apr. 1846 Norway, immigrated 1876). Occupation: Copper miner, farmer. Children: Julia. According to Martin Ulvestad in "Nordmændene I Amerika", "The first Norwegians in this county (Sargent, ND) were the brothers Thomas and Martin O. Hall from Romsdalen. In the beginning of the 1880s, they settled in the area of De Lamere, where a township is named after them."

Hallan, Jonas O. (Jonas Olsen Hallon), b. 27 Jan. 1876 in Aurdal Twp., Otter Tail Co., MN; d. 18 Nov. 1918 Aurdal, Otter Tail Co., MN. Parents: Ole Hallan (1837 Skogn-1924) & Helena Hanan (1840-1927). The father emigrated from Bergen 27 May 1865 on the bark *Præsident Harbitz* and arrived in Quebec 17 July 1965. He was one of many on the ship who listed his residence as Trondhjem.

The mother emigrated about 1873. Lived in Otter Tail Co. Did not marry. Occupation: Farmer with Holstein cattle and Berkshire swine. No children.

Hammer, S.O. (Sivert Olsen Hammer), b. 20 Jan. 1838 Hoe farm, Inderøy, Nord-Trøndelag; d. 29 April 1924 Otter Tail Co., MN. Parents: Ole Hansen Hammer (b. 1803 Inderøy) & Jonetta Aagesdatter (b. 1807 Inderøy). Emigrated 19 May 1869 from Vagan to Chicago, IL leaving on ship *Sweden* from Trondheim. Settled in Otter Tail Co., MN. Married on 27 Dec. 1862 in Norway to Gitlov Elizabeth Marcusdatter (1837-1890). Occupation: Farmer. Children: Hans, Julius, Martin, Caspara, Joackim, Inga, Joseph, Oscar, and Simon Hammer.

Sivert O. Hammer (1838-1924)

Hatling, J. O. (Jacob Petter Olsen Hatling), b. 17 Dec. 1851 Stod, Nord-Trøndelag; d. 1 March 1939 Dalton, MN. Parents: Ole Abrahamsen & Enger Hansdtr. (1834-1905). Emigrated with his mother, step-father (Taral Olsen [Hatling] Rygh) and half-brother Ole Rambek Rygh, in 1865 or 1866 to Decorah, IA. In 1867 the family moved to Dalton, MN. Jacob married 28 June 1871 to Gusta Lorntsdatter Meldahl (1857 Meldahl farm, Stod, Nord-Trøndelag-1940 Dalton, MN). Occupation: Operated a general store with his step-father for several years, then a hardware store with farm equipment. Children: Gustave, John, John, Lewis, Emma, George, Julia, Baby, Noble J., Mae, and Arthur J. Hatling.

Hatlinghus, J. (John Sigurd Staalsen Hatlinghus), b. 11 Oct. 1865 Stod (Steinkjer), Nord-Trøndelag. Parents: Staal Georgius Enertsen Vannebo (b. 1823 Beitstad) & Rebekka Jørgine Pedersdatter (b. 1823 Beitstad). Emigrated 5 June 1907 from Stod with a destination of Fergus Falls, MN. His brother, Peter Stolson, had emigrated to Fergus falls in 1881. Settled first in Fergus Falls, then in Minneapolis by 1920. Did not marry. Occupation: Farmer in Norway, janitor in the U.S. No children.

Hauan, O.C. (Ole Christensen Hauan), b. 22 Jan. 1844 Overhalla, Nord-Trøndelag; d. 16 Dec. 1921 in Santa Barbara, CA. Parents: Christen Larsen Schemoe or Hauan (b. 1812) & Johanna Olsdatter. Emigrated from Overhalla 11 April 1866 under name of Ole Christensen Skomo. Settled in Spring Grove, MN, moved to Trail Co., ND (1878). Married 11 Jan. 1868 in Spring Grove, MN to Kjersti Amundsdatter Lunde (b. 1851 Sør-Aurdal, Oppland; d. 1916). Occupation: Farmer, first Assessor in Mayville Twp, ND, County Commissioner, Representative of State Legislature. Elected Public Administrator and County Coroner. Children: Julia Christine, Albert Levrin, Julia Marie Christene, Bertha Oline, Christian Ingebright, John Marcus, Ole Christian (1894-1895), and Ole Christian (1897-1901) Hauan.

Ole and Kjersti Hauan from Overhalla, Nord-Trøndelag

Haugan, Bernt B. (Bernt Doldus Benjaminsen Haugan), b. 17 Sept. 1862 Skogn, Nord-Trøndelag; d. 5 Dec. 1931 Snohomish Co., WA. Parents: Benjamin Helgesen Haugan (b. 1832 Skogn) & Beret Marie Ellevsdtr. (b. 1824 Skogn). Emigrated 3 April 1872 from Skogn. Settled first in Dakota Territory, then in Fergus Falls, by 1920 in Redfield, SD and by 1930 in Mukilteo, WA. Married (1) abt 1887 to Bettie Hawkanson (b. 1861 MN; d. 1932) and (2) abt 1925 to Grace H. (b. 1871 NY). Occupation: preacher, real estate agent, traveling public speaker. Children with Bettie: Edgar and Elenore Marie (or Marie E.) Haugan.

Haugan, O.B. (Otter Martin Benjaminsen Haugan), b. 9 March 1867 Ekne, Skogn, Nord-Trøndelag; d. 25 May 1924 Otter Tail Co., MN. Parents: Benjamin Helgesen Haugan (b. 1832 Skogn) & Beret Marie Ellevsdtr. (b. 1824 Skogn). Emigrated 3 April 1872 with his family. Brother of Bernt B. Haugan. Settled (1) Dakota Territory (2) Otter Tail Co., MN. Not married. No children. Graduated from

CHARTER MEMBERS

Medical School at Northwestern University in Evanston in 1902. Occupation: Doctor/General Practice in Fergus Falls.

Hindrum, John (Johan M. Nilsen Brubak), b. 4 April 1834 Leksvik, Nord-Trøndelag; d. 4 Nov. 1921 Otter Tail Co., MN. Parents: Nils Olsen Hoven & Anna Larsdatter Brobakken. Emigrated 11 May 1869 from Lexvigen to La Crosse, WI. Settled in Fergus Falls, MN. Married Anna Olava (1844 Norway-1896). Occupation: Farmer. One child: Mary M. Hindrum (b. 1873) who married Martin Nordahl abt 1891 and had five children.

Hogstad, John (John Olsen Hogstad), b. 1852 Hogstad østre, Inderøens, Nord-Trøndelag; d. 1 Feb. 1938 Fargo, ND. Parents: Ole Hansen Hogstad (b. 1814 Inderøy) & Pauline Ingebrigtsdatter (b. 1816 Inderøy). Emigrated 8 March 1883 to America. Settled in Traill Co., ND, Moorhead, MN, and Fargo, ND. Married about 1886 to Marenanna Andreasdatter Berg (b. 24 Oct. 1856) who had also come from Inderøy. Occupation: Cattle buyer, farmer. Children: 2 who died young in America. Marenanna had a son Martin in 1877 with Ole Benjaminsen Aas. The son remained in Norway, living with her parents on the Berg farm in Inderøy.

Huseby, Arnt O. (Arnt Severin Olsen Huseby), b. 10 Dec. 1869 Goodhue Co., MN; d. 9 July 1950 Fergus Falls, MN. Parents: Ole Arntsen Huseby (b. 1895 Vestre Huseby, Nedre Stjørdal, Nord-Trøndelag; d. 22 March 1895 Otter Tail Co., MN) & Berit Johnsdatter Ertsgaard (b. 22 Feb. 1848 Øvre Stjørdal, Hegra; d. 1916). Parents emigrated 29 April 1869 with a destination of Chicago. Family settled in Goodhue Co., then Dane Prairie, Otter Tail Co., MN for 80 years. Arnt married 29 Nov. 1900 to Sina Tvete Opheim (her 2nd marriage), b. 26 Feb. 1871 Norway; d. 19 June 1942 Fergus Falls.

Arnt O. Huseby, born in Minnesota of parents from Nord-Trøndelag

81

Occupation: Farmer. Children: Alfred, Oscar, Sydney Bernard, Robert Amund, and Paul Sigmund Huseby.

Huseby, Severin (Oliver Severin Arntsen Husby), b. 15 May 1855 Vestre Husby, Nord-Trøndelag; d. 5 Dec. 1926 Fergus Falls, MN. Parents: Arnt Gunnarsen Midtkil (Hegra) (1794-1856) & Olivie Hansdtr. Bjerkenplass (1826-1891). Emigrated 22 March 1882 from Nedre Størdalen with a destination of Fergus Falls. Settled in Fergus Falls, Otter Tail Co., MN. Married about 1882 to Bollete (Belle) Torgerson, b. 1 July 1866 Finnmark; d. 1942 Fergus Falls. Occupation: Stone mason, patrolman, police chief. Children: Arthur, Clara, Merriam, and Orville Alfonso Huseby.

Huus, Ulrick (Ulrik Julian Antonsen Sørdero (Huss), b. 22 June 1876 Sør-dryø, Frøya, Sør-Trøndelag; d. 13 April 1953 Minneapolis, MN. Parents: Anton Enoksen Huss Søderø (b. 1831 Hitterens) & Ingeborg Petersdtr. (b. 1841 Hitterens). Emigrated 12 July 1893 from Frøyen to Fergus Falls. Settled in Fergus Falls, then to Fargo, ND by 1918, to Minneapolis by 1930. Married abt. 1898 to Anna Christine Baglo, b. 1878 Værdalen, Norway. Occupation: Sash and door maker, ironmaker, contractor, draftsman in lumber company, Children: Borghild A., Clara A., Clarence, Arnold, Raymond Bernard Huus.

Ingebregtsen, Endre /aka Andrew E. Leren (Endre Ingebrigtssen Leirmarken), b. 29 April 1833 Stjørdal; d. after 1920. Emigrated 16 April 1866 for America with his wife Beret and daughter Martha. Settled first in Goodhue Co., MN; by 1870 in Douglas Co., MN. Married in Norway to Beret Nilsdatter Lerplass, b. 1822 Nedre Størdalen. Occupation:

Left: Endre and Beret Ingebregtsen (Leren) with daughter Martha and her husband Ole O. Johnson and their two children, photo abt 1886-1889

CHARTER MEMBERS

Farmer. Children: Martha, b. 1857 Norway who married Ole O. Johnson from Hallingdal.

Jensen, Jacob (Jakob Elian Jensen Gjessingen), b. 26 March 1866 Sør-Frøien, Sør-Trøndelag; d. Aug. 1973 Minneapolis, MN. Parents: Jens Henrik Johansen (b. 1855 Frøien ST) & Ingeranna Eliasdatter (b. 1858 Frøien ST). Emigrated 17 Sept. 1907 from Kristiania to Fergus Falls, MN. Living at Gjessingen farm in Sør-Frøya in 1900; last residence before emigration: Troms. Settled in Minneapolis, MN. Married abt 1918 to Elvera S. (b. 1896 MN; d. 1991). Occupation: Home decorator and painter. Jacob Jensen was self-taught on the violin and made three violins. One child: Ivan Raymond Jensen, b. 1920 MN.

Jacob and Elvera Jensen

Johanson, Paul /aka Paul Johnson (Paul Rasmus Johansen), b. 17 July 1864 Inderøens, Nord-Trøndelag; d. 13 June 1940 Otter Tail Co., MN. Parents: Johan Jakobsen (b. 1830) & Pauline Rasmusdatter (b. 1838) living at Sakshaug, Inderøen, Vattenplads in 1865. Emigrated 12 June 1883 from Inderøen to Fergus Falls, MN starting out on the feedership Hero from Trondheim. Settled in Fergus Falls area. Never married. No children. Occupation: Farm laborer, farmer.

Johnsen/Johnson, Fred (Fredrik Johannssen Aarønæs), b. 24 June 1848 Bolsøy, Møre og Romsdal; d. after 1920. Parents: Johan Larsen Aarønæs & Ingeborg Hansdatter. Emigrated 28 Aug. 1890 from Bergen with wife and foster daughter. Settled in Wilkin Co., MN, then Fergus Falls by 1905. Married 20 April 1878 at Frænen, Møre og Romsdal to Maren Ellingsdatter (b. 19 March 1860 Frænen). Occupation: Farmer. Foster child: Martine (Tillie) Hoff, b. 14 Nov. 1884 in Molde, Møre og Romsdal.

83

Johnson, Chris aka/ Christian Johnson (Christian Olsen/ Zakariasen), b. June 1851 Sparboen, Steinkjer, Nord-Trøndelag; d. 20 Jan. 1922 Fergus Falls, MN. Parents: Stepfather: Zakarias Jens. Maere, b. 1817 Sparbu & mother Karen Johnsdatter, b. 1827, Sparbu. Emigrated 2 May 1867 from Trondheim on the bark *Franklin* – arrived Quebec 9 June 1867. Settled in Rushford, Fillmore Co., MN (1867-1871), then Otter Tail Co., MN. Married abt 1874 to Eva G. Moe, b. 1858 Norway; d. 1836 Ramsey Co., MN. Occupation: Railway work, clerk in general store, deputy sheriff of Otter Tail County, auctioneer, justice of the peace and real estate business. Children: John S., Carl M., Eleanor, Edward C., Thord M., Cora, Margaret, and Harold Johnson.

Johnson, Martin (Bernt Martin Johnsen (Storvuku), b. 8 Sept. 1864 Storvuku Værdalen, Nord-Trøndelag; d. 6 March 1946 Fergus Falls, MN. Parents: John Johnsen Storvuku (1834 Verdal-1900 MN) & Bereth Marta Syrensdatter/Sørensdatter (b. 1835 Verdal). Emigrated from Trondheim 8 July 1882 with his parents and siblings with a destination of Eau Claire, WI. Family settled in Eau Claire (1882-1890), Fergus Falls (1890-1920) Wilkin Co., MN where Martin farmed 1925-1937. Married 26 June 1890 at Tordenskjold Lutheran Church to Martha Malina Albertson (b. 1870 MN; d. 1945 Fergus Falls). Occupation: Farmer, merchant-second hand store, proprietor of a garage. Children: Martha, Charles Peter Manuel, Albert F., John S., and Betsy M. Johnson.

Bernt Martin and Bereth Johnson

Theo Johnson (1847-1925) outside his Meat Market in Fergus Falls

CHARTER MEMBERS

Johnson, Theodore (Theodor Johannesen Lerfald), b. 17 Nov. 1847 Værdalen, Nord-Trøndelag; d. 11 January 1925 Fergus Falls, MN. Parents: Johannes Hansen Maritvoldvald Øren & Guru Halvorsdatter Maritvoldvald Øren. Living at Leirfald vestre farm in Verdal in 1865. Emigrated from Verdalsøra, Norway 17 April 1870. Went to Eau Claire, WI where he worked in the woods and sawmills. Settled in Fergus Falls in 1875. Married 4 July 1872 in Eau Claire to Martha Cathrina Jensdatter also from Værdalen (1844-1908). Occupation: Owned and operated a butcher shop and meat business in Fergus Falls. Children: Gilmer, Conrad, Sophia (adopted granddaughter) Johnson. *(See photo p. 20)*

Jordahl, Anton (Anton Gerhard Olsen Jordahl), b. 30 Jan. 1864 Kristiansund, Møre og Romsdal; d. 22 Nov. 1945 Zurich, Montana. Parents: Ole Jacobsen Jordahl (b. 1822 Stangviks, Møre og Romsdal) & Lina Olsdatter (b. 1830 Trondhjem). Emigrated 12 May 1888 from Strinda/Trondheim to Spencer, IA, leaving Trondheim on the *Thingvalla*. Anton returned to Norway to bring back his future wife and sisters Amalie & Olise - they emigrated 27 June 1892 to Spencer, IA. Married 30 Dec. 1892 to Caroline Sawert (1865-1934). Settled in Dickinson Co., IA, then to Fergus Falls, MN, and Blaine Co., MT. Occupation: Farmer. Children: Agnes Helen, Sigurd M., Victor H., and Gothleib Olaf Jordahl.

Anton Jordahl about 1890 - his first year in America

Jordahl, Mrs. Caroline (Karoline Helene Sawert), b. 4 Dec. 1865 Trondheim, Norway; d. 17 Sept. 1934 Havre, Montana. Parents: August Friederich Gottlieb Sawert (b. abt 1832 Tydskland) & Ane Catrine (b. abt 1835 Røraas, Sør-Trøndelag). In 1875 the Sawert family was

Anton & Caroline Jordahl in their 1892 wedding photo

85

living in the city of Trondheim. Emigrated with her future husband from Trondheim to Spencer, IA on 27 June 1892. Settled first in Iowa, then Fergus Falls, MN and finally Montana with her husband and family. Children: Agnes Helen, Sigurd M., Victor H., and Gothleib Olaf Jordahl.

Knudsen, Johan (Johan Knudsen Qvamsbak), b. 27 May 1849 Orkedalen, Sør-Trøndelag; d. 2 April 1929 Otter Tail Co., MN. Parents: Knud Sivertsen (b. 1821 Orkdal) & Ane Johnsdatter (b. 1817 Orkdal). Emigrated at age 35 on the feedership *Hero* on 11 April 1882 from Trondheim to Dalton, MN with his wife, Henrikke. Settled in Grant Co., MN and later Fergus Falls. Married 26 Dec. 1872 in Var Frue Kirke, Trondheim to Henrikke Johnsdatter Grue (b. 1844 Norway; d. 1927 Otter Tail Co., MN). Occupation: Farmer. Children: Adopted Christian Grotte, b. 1888 MN and Maria Grotte, b. 1883 MN both of Norwegian parents.

Koefod, Eilert (Eilert Hansen Koefod), b. 12 March 1865 Kristiansund, Møre og Romsdal; d. 4 May 1936 Hill Co., MT. Parents: Hans Koefod (b. 1818 Næsset Prgj.) & Marie Tollefson Koefod (b. 1827 Kristiansund). Emigrated 1882. Settled in Glenwood, MN. Married 21 Sept. 1887 in Glenwood to Klara Rigg (1869-1950). Occupation: Register of Deeds in Pope Co., MN, postmaster in Glenwood, real estate agent in Montana, agent for Algoma Commercial Company who recruited workers in Norway. The company offered "free passage to North America and guaranteed good paid work." Children: Hilmar O., Helen, Ole, Ralph, and Eldred Koefod.

Eilert Koefod (1865-1936)

CHARTER MEMBERS

Lein, Mariane (Mariane Steen), b. 22 April 1862 Stikelstad/Værdalen, Nord-Trøndelag; d. 9 April 1935 Otter Tail Co., MN. Parents: Johan Larsen Thjem & Marith Johnsdatter Forbregdsvald as listed in the birth record in Stiklestad parish. Emigrated 1881/1882. Married Dec. 1883 in Fergus Falls, MN to Peter Lein who also emigrated from Norway. Settled in Fergus Falls. Marianne was one of only eight women who were charter members of Trønderlag. Children: Ben M., Emil, Conrad, and Laura Mercedes Lein.

Mariane Lein (1862-1935) from Stikelstad

Lein, Peter (Peder Pedersen Lein), b. 11 Aug. 1856 Skogn, Nord-Trøndelag; d. 19 Jan. 1927 Fergus Falls, Otter Tail Co., MN. Parents: Peder Olaus Pedersen Leinsval & Bareth Petersdatter. Emigrated from Skogn, Nord-Trøndelag 1879/1880. Settled in Winnipeg, Canada (2 years), then to Fergus Falls. Married Dec. 1883 to Mariane Steen in Fergus Falls. Occupation: Operated butcher shop, then manager/owner of grocery store. Children: Ben M., Emil, Conrad, and Laura Mercedes Lein.

Peter Lein (1857-1927)

Lerfald, O.O. (Ole Olsen Lerfald), b. 15 Feb. 1843 Skogn, Nord-Trøndelag; d. 15 Sept. 1921 Belfield, Stark Co., ND. Parents: Ole Jakobsen Lerfald (1810-1875) & Bereth Anna Andreasdatter Sand (1814-1891). Emigrated 7 May 1866. Settled first in Frazer, Shawano Co., WI, then in Fergus Falls, MN. Married (1) 14 April 1869 in New Denmark, WI to Laura Caroline Christensen (1850 Denmark-1896 MN) and (2) Andreana Thorsten, (b. 1870). Occupation: Farmer, Butcher. Children with Laura: Anton, Oline, Olaff, Anna, John, Julius, Ludwig, Ole, and Elsie Lerfald.

Ole O. Lerfald (1843-1921) from Skogn

87

Rev. S. O. Leirfallom (1872-1927)

Leirfallom, S. O. (Sivert Olsen Lerfold), b. 1872 Østre Leirfall, Hegra, Nord-Trøndelag; d. 27 Aug. 1927 Edmonds, Snohomish, WA. Parents: Ole Iversen Tylden (1835-1906 Hegra) & Sigrd Sivertsdatter Gresset (1838-1928 Hegra). Emigrated 3 April 1889 with his brother John with a destination of Zumbrota, MN. Settled in Brandon, ND (1910), Hickory, MN (1920), Edmonds, WA. Married abt 1908 to Olga Nelson (b. 1886 WI; d. 1976 WA) of Norwegian parents. Occupation: Lutheran Minister. Children: Aslaug, Trond, Jarle, Solveig, Borghild, Alvhild, and Freda Leirfallom.

Lervik, Jon, birth and death dates unknown. Residence in 1908 was Morris, MN. Emigrated from Aas farm in Nedre Stjørdalen according to Trønderlag records. There was no emigration date on the original list while a later document gave the emigration date as 1854. Because there were several Jon/John/Johan Lervik/Lervig, Larvik (and similar spellings) who came to America from Norway, we have not yet been able to determine which one this was.

Loktu, Peter A. (Peter Olaus Antonsen Loktu), b. 2 May 1872 Frosten, Nord-Trøndelag; d. 15 Sept. 1958 Minneapolis, MN. Parents: Anton Arntsen (b. 1832 Frosta) & Marta Marie Jensdatter (b. 1832 Frosta). Emigrated from Trondheim 16 May 1893 using name Peter O. Loktu, age 21, with a destination of Fergus Falls. Settled in Fergus Falls, MN 1893-1920s, Minneapolis, MN 1920s-1958. Married 6 June 1896 in Fergus Falls to Amanda Johnson, b. 1871 Sweden; d. 1940 Minneapolis. Occupation: Carpenter, Fergus Falls Sash & Door company until 1919, then Brooks Bros. in St. Paul. Children: Olga, Minnie Alvida, and Harold Loktu.

Løseth, Mrs. Odin (Astrid Johannesdatter Ekker), b. 18 July 1885 Namdalen, Overhalla, Nord-Trøndelag; d. 2 Feb. 1961 Douglas Co., MN. Parents: Johannes Williamsen Ekker (b. 1855 Overhalla, Skage; d. 1896 Skage) & Marie Andreasdatter (b. 1858 Overhalla; d. U.S.). Emigrated 16 Sept. 1901 from Namdalen to Underwood,

CHARTER MEMBERS

MN under name "Astrid Furun's". (Furrunes was her step-father's name.) Settled in Otter Tail Co., MN. Married abt 1908 to Odin Loseth (b. 1877 MN; d. 1961). Occupation: Homemaker. Children: Orville, J., Myra Charlotte and Helene G. Loseth.

Lund, Edvard (Edvard Torgersen Lund), b. 11 May 1853, Lund, Namsos/Kolvereid, Nord-Trøndelag; d. 5 Jan. 1940 Otter Tail Co., MN. Parents: Torger Baltersen (b. 1797 Lurøy) & Boletta Margrete Andreasdatter Aastøen (1807-1885). Emigrated: 12 June 1889 from Kolvereid to Vining, MN, passage paid in America. Settled in Otter Tail Co., MN. Married 26 July 1909 to Isabella Olson (b. abt 1881). Occupation: Carpenter and contractor. Children: Boletta Margaretta and Ruth Lund.

Mr. & Mrs. Edward T. Lund in Otter Tail County, MN.

Lyng, J. [John] (Johannes Johannesen Lyng), b. 26 Feb. 1870 Lyng mellem østre, Verdalen, Nord-Trøndelag; d. 11 Oct 1935 Otter Tail Co., MN. Parents: Johannes Olsen Lyng (b. 1832) & Karen Marie Andersdatter (b. 1833). Emigrated 11 March 1900 to Underwood, MN. Returned to Norway and emigrated after his wife's death with his three children on 26 Feb. 1906 to Underwood. Settled in Otter Tail Co., MN. Married (1) Oline Gustava Olsdatter Ness (1867-1905); (2) Berit Martha Balgaard (1886-1980). Occupation: Farmer. Children with Oline: Karla Gustava (1893), Olga Johanne (1895), Julie Ottillie (1896), Oskar (1898). Children with Martha: Marius, Borghild, Edna M., Martin, and John Lyng.

Middelfart, Emil (Emil Midelfart), b. 8 Dec. 1875 Trondheim; d. 6 Sept. 1919 Trondheim. Parents: Johannes Unger Midelfart (b. 1833 Drammen) & Katinka Dortkea Kraft (b. 1833 Flekkefjord). Living in Kristiania in 1900. Emigrated in 1906. Married 27 Aug. 1902 in Brevik to Asta Margrethe Schilbred (b. 29 April 1875 Brevik). Occupation: Journalist. Returned to Norway in 1913. Children: Mathias Edvard Schilbred Midelfart, b. 1905 Brevik, d.

89

1968. No descendants. Emil was a descendant of Eidsvolman Hans Christian Ulrich Midelfart, b. 22 July 1772 Bynesset.

From left standing: Emma Ryness, Dina Ryness Nordgaard, John Nordgaard and unknown woman. Seated from left: Selmer Nordgaard, Ella Nordgaard, Bertha Nordgaard, Elvina Nordgaard, Mabel Nordgaard, Stasius Nordgaard and Ellenanne Tollefson Nordgaard.

Nordgaard, Stasius (Henrik Stasius Staalsen Nordgaard), b. 5 Feb. 1831 Stod, Nord-Trøndelag; d. 20 March 1919. Parents: Staal Olsen & Helena Olsdatter, husmannsfolk at Berg in Stod. Emigrated 1 May 1867 from Stod to Quebec with wife Manna and two children. Settled in Otter Tail Co., MN. Married in Norway to (1) Manna Størkersdatter, b. 1826 Stod, d. 1876 MN; and (2) Ellenanna Tollefson, b. 15 Jan. 1827 Norway, d. 1916 MN. Occupation: Farmer. Children with Manna: Staal, b. 1858 and John, b. 1864 Nordgaard.

Nygaard, Ole (Ole Olsen Aune), b. 27 March 1849 Orkdalen, Sør-Trøndelag; d. 10 July 1931 Otter Tail County, MN. Parents: Ole J. Aune (1918 Norway-1901 MN) & Ingeborg (1812 Norway-

1907 MN). Emigrated 1870 to Minnesota. Settled in St. Peter, then Mankato, St. Paul and in 1872 in Sverdrup Twp., Otter Tail Co., MN where he homesteaded. Married 10 Jan. 1882 to Gertrude Sande (b. 1862 Norway) who emigrated in 1882. Occupation: Farmer. Children: Inga, Berntene, Odin O., Olena, Johanna, Alfred, Daniel, Henry O., Ingvald, Mary (Marie), Clarence Nygaard.

Olson, Mads (Mads Olssen Fordalsplads), b. 17 June 1854 Hegra, Nord-Trøndelag; d. 10 Feb. 1937 Detroit Lakes, Becker Co., MN. Parents: Ole Hansen Rotåsen (b. 1807 Hegra) & Maren Anna Ingebretsdatter (b. 1813). Emigrated 11 May 1880 from Øvre Størdalen to Grove City, Minn. Settled in Kensington, MN (one year), Milnor, ND (27 years), then Saskatchewan, Canada (7 years) and finally Detroit Lakes, MN. Married 23 June 1874 in Norway to Gjertrud Pedersdatter (1852-1947) who also joined Trønderlag. Occupation: Farmer. Children: Ole, Anna, Peter Martin, and Ingebright "Bert" Olson.

Mads Olson (1854-1937)

Olson, Olaus (Olaus Olsen Hyndøberget), b. 28 March 1857 Frosta, Nord-Trøndelag; d. 20 July 1933 LaMoure Co., ND. Parents: Ole Ellevsen (b. 1824 Frosten) & Magdalene Eriksdatter (b. 1824 Frosten). In 1865 Olaus, his parents and siblings were living on the Hyndøberget farm in Frosta. Emigrated 18 March 1880 from Frosten to Minnesota. At age 23, he departed on the Dampskib *Tasso*, after paying a fare of 241 spd. and 56 øre. Traveled under name of Olaus O. Hynnevaag. Settled in Blackburn Twp, Litchville, ND. Married 5 Nov. 1885 to Jonetta Sand (1861-1954) who also came from Trøndelag. Occupation: Farmer. Children: John, Anna, Inga, Kjia, Mable, Olga, Ole, and Sigvart Olson. *(See Olaus Olson family photo on next page)*

Olaus Olson, wife Jonnetta Sand and their children (John, Ole, Mary, Annie, Kjia, Inga) on their farm in Blackburn Twp., Litchville, ND

Orstad, Oluf E. (Oluf Ellingsen Aarstad), b. 1 June 1863 Verdalen/Aarstad, Nord-Trøndelag; d. 29 Nov. 1942 Fergus Falls, MN. Parents: Oluf Elling Aarstad (school teacher) & Elen Olsdatter Hallan (b. 1836 Verdal). Emigrated between 1884-1886 from Verdal. He returned to Norway at some point, emigrating again 30 April 1890 to Underwood, MN. Settled in Fergus Falls, MN. Married 1) Gjertrud Lovna Pettersdatter Nesvold (1861-1901) and in 1902 to 2) Olava Romstad (1871 Namsos-1965). Occupation: Carpenter. Children with Gjertrud: Eddie Myer, Alwin Edgar. Children with Olava: Alvin Edgar Orstad.

Overmoen, Lars O. /aka Lewis Olsen (Lars Olsen Overmoen or Ottermo), b. 1 July 1849 farm Ottermoen, Vuku Verdal, Nord-Trøndelag; d. 9 June 1921 Horace, Cass Co., ND. Parents: Ole Lagesen & Margret

Wedding photo of Olaus and Olava Orstad - 1902.

CHARTER MEMBERS

Olsdatter Ottermoe. Emigrated 12 April 1870 from Trondheim. Settled first in Thompson, MN, then Cass County, ND. Married (1) Karen Maria Thomsdal (1849-1889) and in 1891 to (2) Sophia Larsen Sondrall (1868-1925). Occupation: Farmer, postmaster in Warren, ND for 27 years, grain buyer. Children with Karen: Ole Thobias, Anna Matilda, Alfred William, Andreas Leach, Carl Ludvig, Martin Hilbert. Children with Sophia: Arthur Leonard, Mabel, Alice Oline, Melvin Oliver, Lydia Margrete, and Cecilia Lillian Olsen. All went by the surname of Olsen.

Pedersdatter, Gjertru /aka Mrs. Mads Olson, b. 19 April 1852 Trælstad Plassen, Hegra, Nord-Trøndelag; d. 7 Feb. 1937 Detroit Lakes, MN. Parents: Per Olsen Stamnes (b. 1816 Selbu, d. 1857) & Ane Iversdatter (b. 1828 Hegresplass). Emigrated 11 May 1880 from Øvre Størdalen to Grove City, Minn. Settled in Kensington, MN (one year), then Milnor, ND (27 years), then Saskatchewan, Canada (7 years) and finally Detroit Lakes, MN. Married in Norway 23 June 1874 to Mads Olssen Fordalsplads. Children: Ole, Anna, Peter Martin, and Ingebright "Bert" Olson.

Gjertru Pedersdatter (1852-1937)

Pederson, Christ (Kristoffer Pedersen Ydstines), b. 17 Nov 1872 Hegra, Stjørdal, Nord-Trøndelag; d. 14 July 1936. Living in Minneapolis, MN in 1930. Parents: Peder Pedersen Ydstines (b. 1826 Hegra) & Guruanna Pedersdatter Holan (b. 1833 Hegra). Emigrated 4 October 1887 from Størdalen to Minneapolis, MN at age 15. Settled in Minneapolis, MN and Fargo, ND. Married 7 Jan. 1898 in Minneapolis to Nellie T. Flaten (b. abt. 1880 Minnesota). Occupation: Proprietor of a grocery store, organizer of Sons of Norway's Fourth District where he traveled to establish new lodges and sell insurance. Children: Harold T., Arne P., Helen A., and Norman R. Pederson.

Pederson, Nils (Nils Pedersen Grevskot), b. 2 Aug. 1863 Levanger (Landsogn) Nord-Trøndelag; d. 1 April 1852 Fergus Falls, MN. Parents: Peder Nielsen (b. 1813 Levanger) & Bergitte Thoresdatter

93

(b. 1832 Værdalen). Emigrated from Trondheim 6 April 1887 under name of Nils Grevskot, destination Fargo, ND. Settled in Fergus Falls, MN. Married 25 Oct. 1905 in Fergus Falls to Marie Olson (1869-1937). Occupation: Elevator man at a wheat elevator, teamster at a flour mill, janitor at court house. Children: Ragna Norina, May Norina, Belvin Rudolph Pederson.

Peterson, Erik (Erik Pedersen Haarstad), b. 9 July 1866 Rennebu, Sør-Trøndelag; d. 17 Nov. 1949 Richland Co., ND. Parents: Peder Tronsen Haarstad (b. 1813 Rennebu) & Barbro Fredriksdatter (b. 1823 Meldalen). Emigrated 18 April 1888 from Rennebu to Rice Lake, WI with his brother Erik Haarstad, age 25. Worked for two years in the Wisconsin lumber camps before settling in Richland Co., ND. Married in 1891 to Karen L. Bakli (1864-1947) who had emigrated from Orkdal. Occupation: Farmer. Children: Inga Bertina, Peter, and Ida Louise Peterson.

Bertha & Ida, Karen & Erik (Peterson) Haarstad

Petterson, Cornelius (Kornelis Andreas Pedersen), b. 24 Sept. 1831 Karlsøy, Troms; d. 19 July 1921 Otter Tail Co., MN. Parents: Peder Andreasen & Eva Michelsdatter Indrehamre. Emigrated about 1869. A lodger in Vardø, Finnmark in 1865. Married about 1871 to Karen Back (1842 Norway-1911 MN). Occupation: Farmer. Children: Christina P., Edward C., and Peter P. Petterson.

Petterson, Ingolf (Ingolf Theodorson Welde), b. 30 October 1856 Søndre Steinkjer, Nord-Trøndelag; d. 18 March 1934 Pope Co., MN. Parents: Theodor Pedersen Welde (b. 1829 Beitstaden) & Mortine Sivertsdatter (b. 1828 Beitstaden). Emigrated abt. 1875. Settled in Morris, Stevens Co., MN. Married Carrie about 1890. Occupation: House painter. Children: None.

CHARTER MEMBERS

Rathe, Martin (Martin Estenssen Rathe), b. 28 June 1857 Strinden, Lade Parish, Sør-Trøndelag; d. 12 Jan. 1932 Duluth, St. Louis Co., MN. Parents: Esten Olsson Rathe (b. 1822 Strinden) & Karen Anna Simondsdatter (b. 1823 Strinden). Emigrated in 1881, arriving in New York on 23 May 1881 aboard the *SS Furnessia* of the Anchor Line. Settled in Fergus Falls, later in Duluth, MN (by 1930). Married abt 1881 to Sigrid Olsdatter Sneve (1851-1942), also from Strinda/Lade Sør-Trøndelag. Sigrid emigrated 24 Aug. 1881 with brother's wife and children. Occupation: Stone mason. Children: Anna Mathilda, Olaf, Edwin, and Marie Rathe.

Ristad, Ditlef G. (Ditlef Georgson Ristad). b. 22 Nov. 1863 Overhalla, Nord-Trøndelag; d. 20 Sept. 1938 Manitowoc, WI. Parents: George W. Ristad (1830 Overhalla-1904) & Johanna Bergitte Kristiansdatter (b. 1834 Overhalla). Emigrated from Namsos 29 Aug. 1887 with his sister Anna Ristad, age 22;

Ditlef Ristad is pictured standing in the back row (left) above with some of his Ristad and Brøndbo family in Overhalla, Norway in 1904.

destination St. Paul, MN. Moved frequently within Minnesota and Wisconsin to pursue education and then employment opportunities in ministry and education. Married 28 October 1896 in Chicago, Cook Co., IL to Sara/Sarah Moltzau Johnson (b. 1867 Milwaukee). Occupation: Hymnist, professor, pastor, educator, college president. Children: Alf Otto, George Rolf, and Robert Nicholas Ristad. Ditlef Ristad was the primary organizer of Trønderlag of America.

Rønning, B. /aka Fred Ronning (Brynjolf Olsen Rønningen), b. 25 Aug. 1853 Horg, Støren, Sør-Trøndelag; d. 8 Aug. 1936 Breckenridge, MN. Parents: Ole Ingebrigtsen Rønning (1827-1862) & Gollaug Brynjulfsdatter Horgøyen (b. 1825). Brynjolf emigrated in 1880. His mother came to America in 1881. Settled in Chippewa Co., MN, then Milnor, ND. Married 10 June 1888 to Anneta M. Grimsrud (1863-1934) who had emigrated in 1870. Occupation: Farmer. Children: Oliver Alfred, Martin G., Sigward E., and Carl J. Ronning.

Rosvold, Martin (Bernt Martin Rosvold), b. 6 March 1858 Verdal, Nord-Trøndelag; d. 6 Dec. 1942 Otter Tail Co., MN. Parents: Petter Bardoesen Rosvold (1828-1902) & Anna Andersdatter Volen (1836-1896). Emigrated with his mother and siblings 26 April 1869 from Størdalen to Quebec. Left Trondheim on the feeder ship *Franklin*. [The father emigrated in 1867]. Settled in Otter Tail Co., MN in 1870. Lived in Fort Ransom, ND at some point as seven of his children were born there (1889-1898). Married (1) 28 July 1885 to Oline L. Eggen (1868 Norway-1927 MN); married (2) 20 Aug. 1932 in Watertown, SD to Clara Smaagaard (b. 1889) from Lac Qui Parle Co., MN.

Martin Rosvold (1858-1942). Photo from Otter Tail County Historical Museum, Fergus Falls, MN.

Occupation: Farmer. Children with Oline Eggen: Karen Alvilde, Paul Oscar, Astrid, Alfred Ludvig, Nora Alvilde, Anne Katrine, Martha Oline, Olaf Melanchton, Agnes, and Margrette

CHARTER MEMBERS

Rosvold. No children with his second wife.

Røst, Jon (Johan Johannesen Sve), b. 27 Sept. 1867 Leksviken, Nord-Trøndelag; d. 6 Jan. 1934 Moorhead, MN. Parents: Johannes Kristoffersen Hjellupvik Sve (1823-1896 Leksvik) & Beret Dorthea Kristoffersdatter Rian (1834-1908 Leksvik). Emigrated 18 April 1888 to Hawley, MN leaving on feeder ship *Hero* from Trondheim. Settled in Ulen Twp., Clay Co., MN. Married in 1893 to Ellen Marie Swenson from Frosta, Nord-Trøndelag (1860-1930). Occupation: Carpenter. Children: Inga, Oscar Bernard, Clifford, Joseph and Ethel Rost.

From left: Jon Rost, Oliver Rost (nephew), and Oscar Bernard Rost (oldest son)

Rustad, Mrs. O. A. (Anna Othelie Olsdatter Dahl), b. 4 Aug. 1858 Sparbu, Nord-Trøndelag; d. 28 Aug. 1943 Otter Tail Co., MN. Sister of charter member Gunder Dahl, niece of charter member B. C. Dahl, and sister-in-law of charter member Ove Wick. Parents: Ole Kristofersen Dahl & Oline Gundersdatter Olstad (b. 1815 Gudbrandsdal). Emigrated from Bergen to Quebec 6 April 1866 with her mother and siblings. Her father had emigrated in 1865. Settled in Tumuli, Ottertail Co., MN. Married in 1878 in Otter Tail Co. to Oliver Rustad. Occupation: Homemaker. Children: Olga Pauline, Alvin O., George R., Duffy O., William R., Guy V., and Irving R. Rustad. *(See family photo on following page)*

97

The Rustad family, photo taken in 1928. Photo from the Otter Tail County Historical Museum.

Schei, Johannes P. (Johannes Pedersen Schei), b. 17 May 1839 Ytterøen, Nord-Trøndelag; d. 22 Jan. 1916 Otter Tail Co., MN. Parents: Peder Johnsen Schei (b. 1810 Ytterøen) & Jocomina Olsdatter (b. 1815 Ytterøen) who also emigrated to America. Emigrated 1 May 1867 from Verdalen to Quebec with many others from Verdalen, including his future wife. Settled first in Goodhue Co., MN and then Otter Tail Co., in 1870. Married Baroline Bardosdatter Rosvold (1841-1936) on 4 July 1867 in Goodhue Co., MN. Occupation: Farmer in Tordenskjold Twp. Children: Olaf, Julia, Karen, Julius, Joseph, Ole, Martin, John G., Olena, and Julia Schei. Baroline was the aunt of charter member (Bernt) Martin Rosvold. Her parents were Baro Andersen Nestvold (1796-1850) & Kjersti Pedersen Rosvold (1801-1888). Baro took over Rosvold nordre and vestre farms in 1826.

Schei, Ole J. (Olaf J. Schei), b. 9 May 1868 Goodhue Co., MN; d. 19 Feb. 1956 Otter Tail Co., MN. Parents: Johannes P. Schei and Baroline Rosvold. (see above). No emigration. Grew up in

Tordenskjold Twp., Otter Tail Co., MN. Married Signe Vinje
(1877-1948) from Kongsvinger, Norway in 1900. Occupation:
Joined a clothing business in Fergus Falls in 1891, started his own
clothing store in 1899 and retired in 1937 when he sold his business
to St. Clair and Gunderson. Children: Helen J., Russell J., Vernon
Olaf, and Harold W.

Selness, Haakon (Haakon Olausen Selnæs), b. 18 April 1881
Verdal, Nord-Trøndelag; d. 2 Oct. 1965 Fergus Falls, MN.
Parents: Olaus Pettersen Hjeldevald (b. 1842 Verdal) & Kjerdstine
Olsdatter (b. 1845 Verdal). Emigrated 21 April 1903 from Verdalen
to Warren, ND, leaving Trondheim on the feeder ship *Tasso*.
Settled first in Benson Co., ND, but was in Fergus Falls by 1920.
Married (1) in 1915 to Clara Freng (1884- 1918) and (2) in 1923 in
Fergus Falls to Louise Franze (1890-1967). Occupation: Building
contractor. Child with Clara: Clayton. Children with Louise:
Robert Malcolm, Eunice, Rose Marie, and James Selnes/Salnes.

Sjørdal, Theo [Theodore O.] (Theodor Olsen Skjørdal), b. 12 Dec.
1860 Verdal, Nord-Trøndelag; d. 10 April 1923 Underwood, MN.
Parents: Ole Thoresen Skjørdal (b. 1829
Verdal) & Guruanna Johnsdatter Sundby
(b. 1833 Verdal). Emigrated about 1870/71.
Settled in Sverdrup Twp., Otter Tail Co.,
MN. Married 25 July 1885 to Inga Maria
Lein (1863-1905). Occupation: General
merchandise business as well as an elevator
with his brother-in-law Hans Bjorge. When
the partnership ended in 1909, he devoted
time to buying and shipping livestock and
operating a retail meat market in Underwood.
Children: Elmer, Conrad, Richard, Edwin,
Mabel Louise, Hjalmer, Gudrum Eleanor,
and Harold Burdette Sjordal.

*Theodore Olsen Sjordal (1860-1923) and
wife Inga Marie Lein (1863-1905).*

Iver O. Skistad (Iver Olsen Skistad), b. 6 June 1836 in Overhalla, Inderøien Prg., Nord-Trøndelag; d. 18 Nov 1915 Otter Tail Co., MN. Parents: Iver Rasmussen from Bjørnør parish & Ingeborg Hansdatter Wigen. Iver moved from Inderøy to Grong and emigrated to America from Grong in 1866. Took a homestead in Otter Tail Co., MN, close to Elizabeth. Married in 1870 to Norwegian Synneve Halvorsdatter (1844-1914). Occupation: Farmer. Children: Haakon, Ida, Sannah, Sigurd, and Ingvald Skistad.

Skrove, Oline (Oline Margaret Dahl), b. 27 Jan. 1868 near Hesper, IA; d. 7 Feb. 1951 Tumuli Twp, Otter Tail Co., MN. Parents: Børre C. Dahl (1830-1908) & Anna Helena Michaelsdatter Utilvika (Wick). Parents emigrated from Beitstad, Nord-Trøndelag. Lived in Winneshiek Co., IA and Otter Tail Co., MN. Married 28 May 1885 (1) Nicolai Stevny who died in 1889; (2) married 1 Oct. 1893 to Sigurd M. Skrove. Children: Martha, Berton, Neola, Sanford, and Milda,

Oline & Sigurd Skrove on their 50th Wedding Anniversary 1 October 1943.

Skrove, S. [Sigurd] M. (Sigurd Martinussen Skrove) b. 22 April 1867 Verdal, Nord-Trøndelag; d. 11 Nov. 1963 Fergus Falls, MN. Parents: Martinus Ellingsen Skrove (b. 1835 Vuku Verdal) & Martha Jonasdatter (b. 1841 Stiklestad Verdal). Family resided at Skrove øvre østre farm in Verdal with four children in 1865. Emigrated with his parents and siblings, arriving in New York 26 July 1882 on the ship *Hekla*, which left from Christiania and Copenhagen. Settled first in Fergus Falls. Took up a homestead in Wilkin Co., in 1888. Moved to Tumuli Twp., Otter Tail Co., in 1793 when he purchased 250 acres of land. Married 28 May 1893 to Oline Margaret Dahl (1868-1851). Occupation: Farmer. Children: Martha, Berton, Neola, Sanford, and Milda,

Sigurd M. Skrove (1867-1963)

CHARTER MEMBERS

Sneve, O. S. (Ole Svendsen Sneve), b. 17 Feb. 1846 Oppdal, Sør-Trøndelag; d. 1913 Silvana, Snohomish Co., WA. Parents: Svend Svendsen Vikelund (b. 1910 Sweden) & Sigri Olsdatter Sneve (b. 1818 Opdal). Family lived on farm Sneve in Oppdal in 1865. Emigrated 17 May 1871 from Oppdal to La Crosse, WI. Settled in: Brookings, SD (1880), Silvan, WA (1910). Married 1874 in La Crosse, WI to Ingeborg Olsdatter Moen (1851-1920), also born in Opdal. Occupation: Farmer, poet. Children: Klara, Anna Sofie, Severin Carl Martin, Sarah Emelia, Elisabeth, Inge Josefine, and Hans Sneve. Sneve's mother, Sigrid, age 56, emigrated 25 June 1874 from Oppdal to La Crosse with two children. Future wife Ingeborg Moen, age 22, emigrated 7 Aug. 1873 from Oppdal to La Crosse.

Solberg, Olaf A. (Olaf Alfred Solberg), b. 9 Feb. 1872 MN; d. 13 Feb. 1943 Seattle, WA. Parents: Baard Olessen Solberg (b. 1841 Verdal, Nord-Trøndelag; d. 1921 Fergus Falls, MN) & Anne Hansatter Bergdalmoes (b. 1851 Vaga, Oppland; d. 21 Feb. 1929 Fergus Falls). The father, Baard, emigrated from Trondheim on feeder ship *Florence* with his brother Bertinus Olsen 5 May 1867, destination La Crosse, WI. The mother emigrated abt 1868. The family settled in Urness, Douglas Co, MN; Fergus Falls by 1900; Seattle, WA by 1920. Olaf abt 1900/01 married Bertha (Bergeta) Medjaa (1878-1966). Occupation: hotel manager (1900), restaurant proprietor (1910), apartment manager (1930). Children: Raymond, Clifford T., and Mildred Bernice Solberg.

Solem, A. [Anfinn] (Anfind Ellefsen Fredricksted Solem), b. 27 April 1850 Lade Strinden, Sør-Trøndelag; d, 26 June 1933 Otter Tail Co., MN. Parents Ellef Anfindsen (b. 1818 Støren; d. after 1900) & Inger Serine Pedersdatter (b. 1826 Røraas; d. after 1900). Emigrated from Strinden 9 Sept. 1879 with a destination of St. Cloud, MN. Was listed as a "Tekniker" (technical expert). Settled in Pelican Lake, MN (1880), Fergus Falls (from 1880 on). Married Marith Ingebrigtsdatter Rise Rønning (1859-1959). Marith had emigrated from Rise gard, Opdal in 1880. Occupation: Teacher, engineer, publisher of the *Fergus Falls Ugeblad* for 35 years. Graduated from Klåbo seminary near Trondheim in 1870. Taught school for 5 years in northern Norway, then attended polytechnic school in Trondheim for 3 years. Children: Eyvind Anfin (1881-1882), Eyvind Anfin, S. Amalie, Harold, and Synneva Henderson Solem.

Stav, C.P. (Christian Paulson Stave), b. 3 March 1848 Stav vestre, Malvik, Strinda, Sør-Trøndelag; d. 21 March 1925 Aastad Twp., Otter Tail Co., MN. Parents: Paul Carlson Stav (b. 1802 Strinden) & Gunhild Tørkildsdatter. Emigrated 19 May 1870, departing from Trondheim on the *S/S Norway*; destination: Chicago. Settled briefly in La Crosse, WI, then to Goodhue and Rice Counties in Minnesota where he farmed. By 1880 he is in Aastad, Otter Tail Co. Married Kari Knutsdatter (b. 1852, daughter of Knud Olsen Vigen). Occupation: Farmer, merchant. Took his daughter Clara with him to Norway to visit family in 1902. Children: Gurina Cecile, Ingeborg Caroline, Clara Pauline, Ida Caroline, Pasvig Adolph, Mendine Carette, Anna Mathilda, and Louise Malene.

Christian Paulson Stav (1848-1925) from Malvik, Strinda

Stene, B.M. (Bernt Martin Stene), b. 15 Feb. 1867 Verdalen, Nord-Trøndelag; d. 8 Jan. 1963 Otter Tail Co., MN. Parents: Martinus Bardo Østgaardsvald & Berith M. Halstensen. Emigration: 19 April 1893 from Verdalen to New York, on ship *Juno*, departing from Trondheim. Did not marry. Occupation: Carpenter (1900), farm laborer (1920), farmer (1930). No children.

Strinden, Isak (Isak Pedersen Strinden), b. 15 Nov. 1845 Stod, Nord-Trøndelag; d. 15 Apr 1929 Otter Tail Co., MN. Parents: Peder Ingebrigtsen (b. 1816 Stod) & Karen Taraldsdatter (b. 1816 Stod). In 1865 the family was living on the farm Bøle Almending in Stod. Emigrated in 1866 from Stod with his brother Andreas

CHARTER MEMBERS

Strinden (b. 1842). Settled first in Filmore Co., MN, then to Otter Tail Co., in 1870. Married 16 Nov. 1874 to Maren Sophie Thronsdatter Vigen (1852-1939). Occupation: Farmer. Children: Carrie, Lizzey, Theodore, Peder, Teddy Alfred, Ignette Mahilda, and Norman Isak Strinden.

Isak & Sophie Strinden married in 1874

Sumstad, Anton (Anton Olsen Sumstad), b. 18 June 1879 Bjørnør, Sør-Trøndelag; d. 1920-1930. Parents: Ole Olssen Sumstad (b. 1833 Bjørnør) & Ingeborg A. Andreasdatter (b. 1841 Bjørnør). Emigrated 25 May 1898 from Bjørnør to Barret, MN, leaving Trondheim on ship *Juno* with two brothers, Martin & Abraham Sumstad. Settled in Ashby, Grant Co., MN. Married about 1904 to Ella Nelson (1881-1956), daughter of Gustaf & Torgen (Newhouse) Nelson. Occupation: Farmer. Children: Inez T. and Vida E. Sumstad.

Svendsgaard, Thorolf (Thoralf Larsen Svendsgaard), b. 2 Sept. 1871 Kristiansund, Møre og Romsdal; d. 12 May 1945 Elizabeth, MN. Parents: Lars (1829-1908) & Constance (1848-1926) Svendsgaard. Emigrated with his parents about 1881. Settled on a farm in Long Lake, MN in 1883. Married 3 June 1927 to Karina Kopperud (1876-1949) of Pelican Rapids. Occupation: Farmer. No children.

Anton & Ella Sumstad and children Vida and Inez

Svorkmo, N. O. (b. Orkdalen, Sør-Trøndelag), emigrated 1891. Lived in Fergus Falls, MN in 1908 and 1910. Unfortunately we have not been able to determine more about Mr. Svorkmo than the information provided to the Trønderlaget in 1908 and 1910.

Thompson, A. [Anton] B. (Anton Berntsen Thompson), b. 8 Feb. 1870 Grant Co., MN; d. 12 Aug. 1946 Fergus Falls, MN. Parents: Bernt Thomassen Lilleevjen (b. 1822 Selbu) & Ingre Estensdatter Gulseth (b. 1832 Selbu), immigrants from Selbu, Sør-Trøndelag. [See *Trønderlag Aarbok 2005*, pp. 343-345 for further information about his parents.] Parents emigrated 9 May 1866 from Trondheim aboard the ship *Neptunus*. Arrived at Quebec 9 June 1866. Family settled first in Houston County, MN, then in 1869 moved to Dane Prairie Twp., Otter Tail Co., MN. Married in 1897 to Ragnhild Vinje (1873-1954), daughter of Olof O. Vinje. Occupation: Teacher, lawyer, county attorney, Judge of District Court of 7th Judicial District (appointed by Governor Floyd B. Olson). Attended seminary at age 17 at Willmar, MN, 1896 - University of Minnesota Law school. Children: Marion B., Harriet G. Frances V., Innis M., Owen V., Anton R., and Helen M. Thompson.

The A. B. Thompson family - from left, Front: Helen, Anton Thompson, Ragnhild, Anton; Back: Owen, Francis, Marion, Harriet, Innis

Thompson, John (John Thomassen Klevberg), b. 1 Dec. 1856 Stjørdal; d. 24 April 1937 Douglas Co., MN. Parents: Thomas Halvardsen Klevberg (b. 1824 Selbu) & Ane Thomasdatter Klevberg (b. 1850). Emigrated with his parents on 22 April 1865. Family settled in Fillmore Co., MN (1870), Douglas Co., MN (1880). Remained in Brandon, MN. Married Beret Anna (b. abt 1856; d. 1941). Occupation: Farmer. Children: Tilda, Cora, Cami, Anna, Lena, Nethi, George, and Maggie Thompson.

CHARTER MEMBERS

Thompson, John B. (John Berntsen Thompson), b. 4 Nov. 1876 Dane Prairie Twp., Otter Tail Co., MN; d. 27 Aug. 1929. Brother of Anton and Nels Thompson. Parents: Bernt Thomassen Lilleevjen (b. 1822 Selbu) & Ingre Estensdatter Gulseth (b. 1832 Selbu), immigrants from Selbu, Sør-Trøndelag. Parents emigrated 9 May 1866 from Trondheim aboard the ship *Neptunus*. Married 23 June 1901 to Pauline Tjostelson, daughter of Peter Tjostelson. Occupation: Attorney in Battle Lake, MN; organized Battle Lake Milling Company; became an agent for a popular line of automobiles. Attended school at Willmar Seminar, Luther College and University of Minnesota. Child: Adopted daughter Dorothy.

John B. Thompson (1876-1929)

Thompson, Nels B. (Niels Berentsen Lilleevjen), b. 26 March 1862 Selbu, Sør-Trøndelag; d. 4 May 1941 Otter Tail Co., MN. Parents: Bernt Thomassen Lilleevjen (b. 1822 Selbu) & Ingre Estensdatter Gulseth (b. 1832 Selbu). Brother of John and Anton Thompson. Emigrated 5 May 1866 from Trondheim on the Bark *Neptunus* with his parents and siblings. Settled in Houston Co., MN briefly before setting out in 1869 for St. Olaf Twp. in Otter Tail Co. Nels was one of

The Nels B. Thompson family from left front: Alfred, Wilhelmina, Nels, Ella; Back: Alfred, Theodore, Kermit, Conrad, Norris

105

the sons who walked from St. Cloud to Dane Prairie Twp, helping herd cattle. Married Wilhelmina Bondy 8 Sept. 1891. Occupation: Worked at many jobs as a young man (drove cattle to Winnipeg, worked with livestock, worked on steamboat *Selkirk*, worked on rebuilding of mill dam at Parkdale. Bought his father's farm in Dane Prairie in 1891 and lived rest of life there. Children: Ellen, Alfred B., Conrad I., Wilhelm, Norris N., Theodore M., and Kermit Thompson.

Trøen, Benjamin (Benjamin Pettersen Storvestreplads), b. 5 Dec. 1852 Stod (Forr), Nord-Trøndelag; d. 8 Nov. 1949 Starbuck, MN. Parents: Petter Rafael Andersen Storvestreplads (b. 1818 Stod) & Marta Benjamindsdatter (b. 1824 Sparboen). In 1865 Benjamin was living at Klæbo farm in Stod; parents were living at Trøen farm. Emigrated with his parents 28 April 1871. In 1880, the family is living in White Bear Lake, Pope Co., MN. Married 23 Nov. 1882 to Hannah Hatling (1859-1963) who emigrated with her parents (Michael Petersen & Olava Morthensdatter Hatling) from Stod in 1866. Occupation: Farmer. Children: Marie, Peter, Olava, Ellen, and Magnus Troen.

Trovaten, Mrs. A.A. aka/Betsy Hanson (Berith Hansdatter Lillemo), b. 21 Oct. 1865 Vestre Lillemo, Lånke, Nord-Trøndelag; d. 1946 Barnesville, ND. Parents: Hans Peter Hansen Lillemo (1840 Lånke-1890 Brandon, MN) & Gunhild Torsteinsdatter Julset (1842 Lånke-) Emigrated with parents and siblings 25 April 1866 from Trondheim to Quebec on ship *Victor*. Settled in Brandon, Douglas Co., MN. Married Esten (Austin) A. Trovaten (1860-1927) on 24 Sept. 1887 in Cass Co., ND. A. A. Trovaten published the *Fargo Posten*, *Vesten,* and *Fram* newspapers. Occupation: Dressmaker, cook, homemaker. Children: Stillborn girl, Helga, Henry A., Ben, Frithjof, Clifford, Ida, and Theodore Marven Trovaten.

CHARTER MEMBERS

Vigen, Dr. Jorgen G. (Jørgen Gundersen Vigen), b. 20 Sept. 1864 Selbu, Sør-Trøndelag; d. 1 May 1937 Otter Tail Co., MN. Parents: Gunder Jørgensen Vigen (b. 1844 Selbu) & Sigri Pedersdatter (b. 1841 Selbu). Family living on Nervig farm in Selbu in 1865. Emigrated 4 May 1869 from Trondheim with his parents, departing on the *Neptunus* with a destination of "Kvebek". Family settled in Wanamingo, Goodhue Co., MN, to Marshall Co. (1883). Occupation: Physician. Attended Red Wing Seminary, high school in St. Paul, 3-year medical course at University of Minnesota. Practiced medicine first in Lac Qui Parle Co., then Fergus Falls starting in 1896. Married abt 1905 to Martha A. Bartelson (1878-1946). At retirement in 1928, moved to Los Angeles, CA. Children: Harold D. and James H. Vigen.

Dr. Jorgen Vigen (1864-1937)

Wangberg, Pastor Johan O. (Johan Ardt Olesen Vangbergtrø), b. 30 May 18872 Frosten, Nord-Trøndelag; d. 15 Aug. 1965 Council Bluffs, Pottawattamie, IA. Parents: Ole Jakobsen (b. 1835) & Ingebor Anna Larsdatter (b. 1836). Emigrated in 1891, arriving at Port of New York on 13 Feb. 1891 aboard the *City of Berlin*, traveling under name of "Lorents Olsen" (his older brother), destination Illinois. An uncle in America (Lorents Jacobsen Wangberg) had sent his older brother a ticket but Johan used it instead. Settled in Chicago, the uncle's farm in Onawa, IA, then MN, ND, IA. Theology student at St. Olaf College (1900). Married 28 June 1906 Soldier, Monona Co., IA to Hilda Oline Nordby (1872-1953). Occupation: Lutheran Minister. Children: Martha J., (Gilmer) Orlando, Judith Hermia, and Reuben Arnold Wangberg. Sons Reuben and Orlando became Lutheran ministers.

Johan O. Wangberg and Hilda Nordby on 28 June 1906.

107

Wick, Iver M. (Iver Johan Mikalsen Uttervik), b. 4 Dec 1831 Beitstad, Nord-Trøndelag; d. 8 Sept. 1912 Fergus Falls, MN. Parents: Michael Hansen Yttervik (b. 1806) & Olava Andreasdatter, b. 1807 Beitstaden. Emigrated with his wife and family 7 May 1869 from Namsos on the *New Brunswick*. The mother, Olava Wick, emigrated with son Ove in 1866. Settled in Tumuli Twp., Otter Tail Co., MN. Married in 1864 to Adreanna Torbergsdatter Sannan, b. 4 April 1829, daughter of Torber Johnsen cotter at Sanden and Kirsten Johnsdatter. Occupation: Farmer, carpenter. Children: Martin Odin, Tella Karoline, Anna Julia, anna Elsie, and Mina Kalaate Wick.

Wick, Ove (Ove Mortinus Michaelsen Uttervik), b. 3 July 1841 Uttervig, Beistaden (Solberg), Nord-Trøndelag; d. 31 May 1909 Fergus Falls, MN. Parents: Michael Hansen Yttervik (b. 1806) & Olava Andreasdatter, b. 1807 Beitstaden. Emigrated 7 April 1866 with his mother Olava Uttervik, age 58. Brother of Iver Wick. Sister Anna Wick married charter member Børre Dahl. Settled first in Alexandria, Douglas Co., MN, Minneapolis, then Fergus Falls. Married before 1869 to Randina O. Dahl (1842-1898). Occupation: Carpenter, painter. Children: Otella, Clevie, Minnie, Gustav Adolph, Roy A., and "Baby" Wick.

Wigen, T.C. (Torsten Karstensen Viken) b. March 1847 Frostens, Nord-Trøndelag; d. June 1916. Parents: Karsten Torstensen (b. 1821 Frostens) & Karen Halvorsdatter (b. 1821 Frostens). In 1865 living on farm Juberg østre in Frosta. Emigrated 15 April 1869 from Frosten to Lansing, leaving from Trondheim on the ship *Norway*. Settled in Otter Tail Co., MN. Married about 1874 to Gurine (1829-1914) who was also born in Norway. Occupation: Farmer, day laborer. No children.

Winkjer, Gunder (Gunder Tomasen Vinkjær), b. 27 Feb. 1840 Vinkjeer farm, Skogn, Nord-Trøndelag; d. 13 July 1934 Douglas Co., MN. Parents: Thomas Larssen Vinkjær (b. 1810 Øvre

CHARTER MEMBERS

Størdalens) & Marith Gundersdatter (b. 1812 Nedre Størdalens). Emigrated 18 April 1860 to Australia and New Zealand where he searched for gold with three or four others from Skogn. Returned to Norway a few years later. Emigrated again abt 1864/65 leaving from Levanger. Settled in Douglas Co., MN by 1900. Married 1867 to Karen Anna Josiasdatter Helle (1850-1913). Occupation: Farmer. Children: Johan Taulo, Peter Joel, Jonetta, Jonetta, Anne Maria, Gideon, Lena, Jonathan, Josias, Theodore G. and Kraft Winkjer.

Gunder T. Winkjer (1840-1934)

Wist, Johannes B. (Johannes Racinus Benjaminsen Wist), b. 6 April 1864 Sund farm, Sakshaug, Inderøy, Nord-Trøndelag; d. 1 Dec. 1923 Decorah, Winneshiek Co., IA. Parents: Benjamin O. Johannessen Wist (b. 1929 Sparbu) & Magdalene Arnoldsdatter (b. 1836 Ytterøens, d. 1866). Living on Sund farm in Inderøy in 1865. Age 20, under name "Johannes Vist" emigrated from Stenkjær 30 April 1884, departing from Trondheim on the Dampsk. *Hero*. Arrived at the Port of New York 23 May 23 1884 aboard the *State of Georgia*, from Glascow. He was listed as a teacher from Norway. Settled in Granite Falls, MN (1900) Decorah, IA (before 1910). Married Josephine Aasve (b. 1859). Occupation: Journalist, author, teacher. Editor of the *Decorah Posten* 1900-1923. Author of *The Rise of Jonas Olsen, A Norwegian Immigrant's Saga*, originally published in Norwegian in the 1920s. Children: Clara, Benjamin Othello, Anne Gurine, and Joseph Wist.

J. B. Wist (1864-1923)

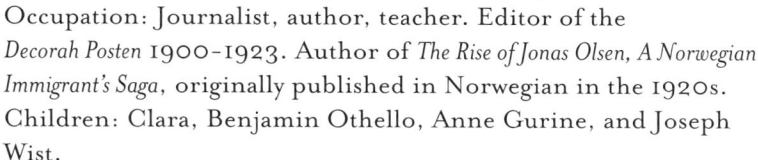

Wold, Einar (Einer Olsen Vold), b. August 1857 Rennebu, Sør-Trøndelag; d. 1933 Richland Co., ND. Parents: Ole Einersen Vold (b. 1817 Rennebu) & Ane Larsdatter (b. 1821 Rennebu). Emigrated with his parents and sister 10 May 1877 from Rennebo to Breckenridge, MN, leaving Trondheim on the Dampsk. *Tasso*.

109

Settled in Abercrombie, ND area. Married 22 May 1882 to Liv Reine (1859-1932), born in Telemark. Occupation: Managed a general store, postmaster in Galchutt, ND and Justice of the Peace. Children: Olga, Christine, Laura, Elnora, Lillian, Clarence, Oscar, and Sylvia Wold.

Wollan, Casper T. (Caspar Thomas Benjaminsen Forrplads), b. 5 May 1848 Stod (Forr) Nord-Trøndelag; d. 16 Aug. 1924 Pope Co., MN. Parents: Benjamin Olsen Forrplads (1795-1879) & Berit Andersdatter Støen (1800-1881). Brother of charter member Michael Wollan. Family signed out of the parish to emigrate to America 7 May 1860 under the name Forrplads. Settled first in Allamakee Co., IA, then Fillmore Co., 1868 in Glenwood, Pope Co., MN. Married 10 Jan. 1875 to Ingebor A. Aal, who emigrated from Norway in 1866. Occupation: Retail merchant, hardware store and tin shop, business manager and treasurer of the Fremåd Association — a large general merchandise store called Wollan Brothers store — organized by the Wollan family in 1874. Children: Margaret, Gustav B., Cornie, Oscar C., Arnold O., Blanch I., Winfred A., Casper I., Clara, and Pernelle T. Wollan.

Casper T. Wollan (1848-1924)

Wollan, Michal A. (Michael Anton Benjaminsen Forrplads), b. Jan. 1844 Stod (Forr) Nord-Trøndelag, d. 30 Jan. 1930 Pope Co., MN. Parents: Benjamin Olsen Forrplads (1795-1879) & Berit Andersdatter Støen (1800-1881). Brother of charter member Casper T. Wollan. Family signed out of the parish to emigrate to America 7 May 1860 under the name Forrplads. Settled first in Allamakee Co., IA, White Bear Lake, Pope Co., then Glenwood, MN (1880-1930). Married about 1871 (1) Isabell A. Rigg (1851-1884); about 1885 (2) Hilma Koefod, (1861-

M. A. Wollan (1844-1930)

1954). Occupation: Engaged in hardware business with his brother Casper, which became Wollan Brothers in 1874; school teacher; president of Pope County State Bank; county auditor; Minnesota state legislature 1877-1887; board of Norwegian Lutheran Synod and Luther College. Children with Isabell: Bertha S., Dorthea S., Sophie M., Josefine W., Oliver Bertram, and Mabel Wollan. Children with Hilma: Holger, Elsie, Margot, and Erling Wollan.

Wollan, T. C. (Thomas Carl Wollan), b. 14 Oct. 1866 Highland Prairie, Fillmore, MN; d. 30 Dec. 1932 Fargo, Cass Co., ND. Parents: Ernst Olaus Wollan (b. 1830 Stod, Nord-Trøndelag, d. 1906) & Bergitta Berg (b. 1827 Stod, Nord-Trøndelag, d. 1911). Parents probably emigrated between 1858-1860. Resided in Pope Co. until after 1900, then Fergus Falls, and Moorhead, MN (1910-1932). Married abt. 1901 to Caroline Gjerset (1878-1957), daughter of Ole S. Gjerset and Karen Marie Eidem. Caroline was sister to charter member Albert Gjerset. Occupation: Superintendent of Schools in Pope Co., MN, professor at Park Region Lutheran College, professor at Concordia College, Moorhead. Children: Ernest, Eunice Lucille, Clarice Amanda, Helen, Margaret, Abner W., and Ralph Orrall Wollan.

Prof. T. C. Wollan (1866-1932)

Living Charter Member Descendants

The search for descendants began in January 2006. Letters were sent to newspapers where the Charter members had indicated they resided in 1908. The responses to the articles in the newspapers were the start of the research. Many hours were spent at the Minnesota Historical Society in St. Paul, the LDS Library in Salt Lake City and online obtaining death certificates, obituaries and Norwegian parish records, contacting local historical societies, libraries, reviewing county history books and WPA Interviews. The Internet has opened up a sometimes faster world of research including the online censuses up to 1930, many birth and death indexes and current online obituaries which were a great help in finding families and descendants.

Contacting descendants by mail or phone and asking for family information, photographs and their own list of descendants was the final step. Charter Member researchers included John Andrisen, Margit Bakke, Mary Benson, Teri Bevan, Barry Dahl, Julia Dixon, Joanne Englund, Carol Greseth, Elaine Hasleton, Nancy Hawkinson, Jo Anne Sadler, Maxine Sandvig, Linda Schwartz and Darlene Stadsvold as well as others who answered online queries, sent us obituaries, photos and other bits of information that aided in our searches.

Some Charter Members did not marry or have children. Some proved elusive. The following is as complete a list of living descendants as we could compile by our publication deadline. Most of these names were provided by Charter Member descendants.

Martin Aalberg: Richard M. Aalberg, Todd R. Aalberg, Kalen Aalberg, Anaya Aalberg, Debra L. Aalberg, Howard Swenson, Elizabeth A. (Swenson) Ring, Carol (Ring) Erickson, Amanda Erickson, John Erickson, David Ring, Sarah Smith, Cassie Wickham, Ruth Mathieu

C.[Cornelius] L. Aasnes: Marie Davis, Karen & Larry Lindquist, Beverly Buness Lindberg, Brad R. Lindberg, Carol Aasnes

Living Descendants of Charter Members

Domke, Timothy A. Domke, Zach Domke, Emerson Domke, Troy P. Domke, Todd M. Domke, Maurice S. Buness, Mary Ann Buness Phillipps, Michelle Buness Jabusch, Louise Buness Madsen, Michael S. Buness, Marvin S. Buness, Marie Buness Davidson, Mark S. Buness, Matthew S. Buness, Stanton C. Stover, Charlene Stover Roning, Paul D. Roning, Heather Roning Wallace, Charles W. Stover, Brandon Stover, Brent Stover, Timothy A. Buness, Oliver M. Buness, Terry L. Buness, Debra Buness Prunella, Randal L. Buness, Vickie Buness Taylor, Monty R. Buness, Laurel Aasness Malmstrom, Daniel P. Malmstrom, Scott J. Malmstrom, Brooke M. Malmstrom, Milton M. Aasness, Pamela D. Aasness Hanson, Brent Hanson, Sara Hanson, Susan K. Aasness Peterson, Tiara Peterson, Malia Lehnertz, Bennett Weisz, Sharon L. Aasness Benson, Debra Benson, Jarrett Benson, Debra J. Aasness Wynn, Adam Wynn, Alyssa Wynn, Junice Aasness Sandness, Kari A. Sandness Whittier, Alex Whittier, Ben Whittier, Kristen R. Sandness Hastings, Kelly Munroe, Julie C. Sandness Wellnitz, Hayden Nelson, Ralph Nelson, , Mary Ann Aasness Quitno, Kristy L. Quitno Harrison, Chelsea Harrison, Trent Harrison, Reece Harrison, Tracy A. Quitno Anderson, Lauren Anderson, Kyle Anderson, Molly M. Quitno Rost, Sami Rost, Jake Rost, Elise Rost, Paul D. Aasness, Perry D. Aasness, Grace Aasness, Ava Aasness, Pearl L. Aasness Ferrin, Curtis Ferrin, Luke Ferrin, Peter P. Aasness, C9onnor Aasness, Megan Aasness, Peggy R. Aasness Skon, Cameron Skon, Brennan Skon, Alison Skon, Sonja Aasness Johnson, Randall D. Johnson, Payton Johnson, Riley Johnson, Cole Johnson, Darrin R. Johnson, Hannah Johnson, Sam Johnson, Sonja Johnson, Renae C. Johnson Strand, Mackenzie Strand, Bailey Strand, Katelyn Strand, Catherine J. Johnson, Janet Aasness Skramstad, Sarah Skramstad, Judy Aasness Dickerson, Deborah L. Dickerson, Richard P. Dickerson, James L. Aasness, Cordelia Hansen Dozier, Ruth E. Hansen, Janice Aasness Riewer, Jon M. Riewer, Phillip R. Riewer, Ame J. Riewer, Nick E. Riewer, Elaine Aasness Kronberg, Owen M. Aasness, Glenda Aasness Ellingson, Terry M. Aasness, Joyce Aasness Kackmann, Arlin M. Aasness, Richard D. Aasness, Marie Aasness Davis, Karen Aasness Lindquist, Ruth Hanson

Ingebrigt H. Aune: No children

Nicolai Baglo: Carl R. Baglo, Doris Baglo, Robert M. Baglo, Jr., Steven & Teresa Coen, Charles Baglo, John D. Baglo, Joseph Baglo, Nicholas Baglo, Stacy Baglo, Jesse Baglo, Gloria Anderson, Mary Kay Strenke, Kevin Strenke, Bradley Strenke, Daniele Strenke, Douglas Strenke, David Strenke, James Strenke, Tanya Foster, Susan Marie Nibbe, Stanley Baglo, Scott Baglo, Talia M. Baglo, Dalton S. Baglo, Sandee M. Harris, Bailey M. Harris, Sherri Lynn Harris, Jacob R. Harris, Dustin M. Harris, Bradley Baglo, Sandra T. Bachman, Kaitlin Bachman, Emily Bachman, Nicholas C. Baglo, Kyle N. Baglo, Claire L. Baglo, Jessica L. Baglo, Ashleigh M. Tammershauser, CJ Tammershauser, Anna Rose Baglo, Joseph J. Baglo, Sarah Lynn Harris, Rachel Labrie, Zachary Labrie, Victoria Labrie

Carl P. Bye: No children

Hans Bye: None found

Johs. E. [Johan Edvard] Bye: Donald R. Carlson, Diane Bye Machande, Dan Machande, Ken Machande, Karen Lambrecht

J.M. [John M.] Bye: Dr. John L. Ellingboe, John W. Ellingboe, Kirsten Orahood, Karen Ellingboe, Bruce Ellingboe, Ann Greville, Mary Masterson, John Masterson, Casey Masterson

B.C. (Borre Christofersen) Dahl: Sidney Skrove, Wyonne Adamsen, Leona Zimmerman

Gunder Dahl: Ann M. Dahl Schwarzwalter, Jane Schwarzwalter, Tim Dahl, Sue Dahl, Linda Dahl Rollison

I. [Ingebrigt] Dorrum: Christian Paul & Elizabeth Preus, Nicholas Eric Preus, Robert & Linda Haines, Mark Haines

Ole Ecker: Harriet Stockman Stickler, Robert Stickler Jr., Lawrence Stickler, Karen Cody, Elton Stickler, Mike Stickler, Debbie Stickler, David Stickler, James Stickler, Perry Stockman, Elizabeth Stockman Walsh, Hannah Ecker Carlson, Olympia Ecker Jenson

Living Descendants of Charter Members

Ole Eidem: No children

O.P. (Ole Paulson) Einan: Armond O. Paulson, Joanne Mitzo, Marcia Rouse, John Paulson

Per Ekker (Perry Ecker): Blaine Ecker, Daryl Ecker, Craig Ecker, Craig Ecker, Daryl Ecker, Judy Glorvigen, Susan Pardy, Greg Ecker, James Ecker, Phillip Ecker, Linda Kronemann, Karen Jyrkas, Dorothy Ecker Landberg, Robert Landberg, Jeffrey Landberg, Paul Landberg, Peter Dewitt Landberg, Michele Kort, Ellen Ecker Johnson, Scott E. Johnson, Derek E. Johnson, William Ecker, Joel Ecker, Kyle Ecker, Barbara K. Ecker, Linda Jean Ecker, Kathleen St. Martin, James Gustafson, David Gustafson, Laurel Porter, Randy Ecker, Kris Strobeen, Terry Ecker, Elizabeth Ecker Wiese, Rosanne Meland, Bradley Wiese, Sheralyn Emery

Jens Eliasen: Barbara Carroll, Rheta Westad Prigge, Phyllis Prigge

Miss Laura Eng: No children

Ole Engen: Marie Engen Wilson, Scott E. Wilson, Ryan Wilson, Sarah Wilson, Douglas & Deborah Wilson, Julie M. Wilson, Tracy A. Wilson, Kimberly M. Wilson, Thomas C. Wilson, Mark R. Laurance, Myles Laurance, Braden Laurance, Logan Laurance, Glen Alan Laurance, Brian Engen, Arthur R. & Anne Engen, Sylvia Conyers, Kimberly Jo Conyers, Kelly L. Conyers Seldowitz, Kim Faber, Dallas Engen, Elizabeth Engen Starner, Madeline Starner, Kayleen Starner, Matt Engen, Brent Engen, Trevor Engen, Karen M. Stovall, Jon E. Wilson, Gertrude Engen Charles, John S. Charles, Randy D. Charles, Alex Charles, Norma Engen, Dallas R. Engen, David K. Engen, Thomas J. Engen, Susan L. Walker, Kyle Walker, Richard Walker, Serena Walker, Christina E. Ibrahim, Kevin Ibrahim, Alexander Ibrahim, Jacqueline Ibrahim, Matthew Ibrahim, Philip L. Engen, David K. Engen, Chris Engen

Peter Enokson: No children

Ole S. Estvold: Doreen Quale & Gary Knutson, Todd & Michelle Knutson, Justin Knutson, Kyle Knutson, Cheryl Knutson, Brad & Jenny Knutson, Austin Knutson, Cole Knutson, Kendra Knutson, Troy & Kallie Knutson, Cooper Knutson, Carter Knutson, Kaiser Knutson, Keith & Audrey Quale, Kolby Quale, Kevin Quale, Kaci (Quale) & Randy Hutzenbiler, Bryce & Jacki Quale, Tyler Quale, Ryan Quale, Lori Quale Renbarger, Derek Maattala, Ethan Renbarger, Steven Quale, Lea Quale, Adrian Estvold, Alan Curtis Estvold, Nancy Hagen, Bruce Estvold, Scott Estvold, Richard & Artus Estvold, Curtis Estvold, Bernice Estvold Rice, Wayne A. Rice, Jessica Rice, Christopher Rice, Andrew Rice, Jonathan Rice, Kathleen Oksendahl, David Oksendahl, Christine Paymon Farazi, Maren Farazi, Patricia Conlon, Paul Conlon, Elizabeth Conlon, Margaret Estvold, Duane & Sharon Estvold, Lisa Estvold, Patty Estvold, Joe Estvold, Vicky & Jim Dawson, Sandy & Barry Johnson, Carol & Brad Zacher, Dale & Holly Estvold, Gloria Estvold, Esther Estvold, Terrance Estvold, Patrick Estvold, Meghan Estvold, Colette Riely, Nathan Riely, Katie Riely, Charise & David Waind, Benjamin Waind, Matthew Waind, Daniel Waind, Lynn Estvold, Troy Estvold, Samuel Estvold, Brian Estvold, Jay Estvold, Ann Estvold, Renae (James LeBrasseur) Estvold, Sydney LeBrasseur, Emily LeBrasseur, Lori (James LeBrasseur) Estvold, Tara Le Brasseur, Kate LeBrasseur, Eric LeBrasseur, Orville E. Estvold, Bob Branch, Don Estvold, Erma Estvold, Randolph Estvold, Greg & Jackie Estvold, Travis Estvold, Marc & Pam Estvold, Nicholas Estvold, Cindy & Greg Estvold, Rait Estvold, Rio Estvold, Frances A. Engen, Karen & Ray Larson, Faith Larson, Robert & Verna Sonmor, Richard & Patricia Sonmor, Roger Sonmor, Charles A. Sonmor, Michael K. Sonmor, Deborah D. Freedlund, Joshua Freedlund, Nathan Freedlund, Kimberly D. Woehl, Brenden Woehl, Evan Woehl, Leanne Sonmor, Dawn Sonmor Odneal, Krista Dawn Odneal, Hannah Odneal, Donald Odneal, Lisa Odneal Redd, Luke Redd, Teri Redd, Olive Marie Sonmor, Jensen, Linda Marie Byrd, Christopher & Kim Byrd, Dustin Byrd, Samantha Byrd, Logan Byrd, Laura Byrd, Colten Hoff, Chase Hoff, Robin Lynn Hoppe, Rebecca Raj, Anthony Raj, Gregory Rag, Kaitlyn

Living Descendants of Charter Members

Hoppe, Claudia & Roger Lund, Serena & Wayne Jiskra, Lindsey Jiskra, Gavin Jiskra, Sarah & Shaun Erickson, Shana Erickson, Brandon Erickson, Ryan Kyle Lund, David Lund, Candace & Keith Simar, Faith Ann & Joseph Kimbler, Jack Kimbler, Maren Kimbler, Nathaniel Simar, Bethany & Kevin Jacobs, William Jacobs, Nathan Jacobs, Franklin & Anita Jensen, Kersten Jensen, Angela & Thomas Foster, Thomas & Dee Dee Foster, Ellie Foster, Joseph & Irene Foster, Dirks Foster, James Foster, Jordan Foster, Michelle Rae Sonmor, Pamela Kubitz Sonmor-Wintz, Dean Allen Sonmor, William Kenneth Sonmor, Harold George, Paul & Judy Sonmor, Marc Sonmor, Larry Sonmor, Christopher Sonmor, Annette Marie Sonmor, Megan Holly Sonmor, Jon Karl Sonmor, Jordan Sonmor, Jennifer Lynn Sonmor, Sally Olinda Spitsberg, Dale & Alice Spitsberg, Heather Jo Erickson, William Erickson, Torin Erickson, Susan & Dan Pickarski, Alisha Pickarski, Kevin Pickarski, Robin R. & Elizabeth Spitsberg, Matthew R. Spitsberg, Kelsey Marie Spitsberg, Craig M. Tabyanan, Janet E. Miller, Mark B. Miller, Madeline Miller, Elizabeth Miller, Wayne (Pamela) Estvold, Tamara Lewis Barnes, Lauren Barnes, Austin Barnes, Addison Barnes, Wesley (Katherine) Estvold, Ethan Estvold, Emma Estvold, Holly (George) Gonzales, Adam Gonzales, Megan Gonzales, Kristin Gonzales, Joshua Gonzales, Shirley & Robert Jensen, Desta & Richard Lutzwick, Eric John Lutzwick, Taylor Marie Lutzwick, Eric J. Lutzwick, Joni R. Jensen, Michael R. Jensen, Gregory E. & Sandra Sonmor, Chad E. (Katie) Sonmor, Shelby Sonmor, Ethel Estvold Beckman, Michaelene (Donald) Flasch, Michael Flasch, Kevin Flasch, Dennis Beckman, Stefan Beckman, Gary L. Beckman, Bryce Beckman, Deborah (James) Cockrell, Jonathan Cockrell, Bill & Becky Sonmor, Sharyn Estvold Hasselbring, Evandah Estvold, Kim Brezinsky, Bill & Lynn Brezinsky, Alyssa Brezinsky, Tyler Brezinsky, Maxine & Bill Rogers, Randall Rogers, Bradley & Judy Estvold, Jonathan & Tiffany Estvold, Kendal & Susan Estvold, Nick Estvold & Matthew Estvold, Jeffrey & Danielle Estvold, Leann & Mark Campbell, Aaron & Cindy Ellickson, Aidan Ellickson, Andrew & Lora Ellickson, Lars Ellickson, Leah Ellickson, Jim Craft, Karrie Craft, Milda Johnson

Jens O. Fossen: Marian Anderson Kubitz, Pamela Kubitz Bice, Nancy Kubitz Larson, Tyler Larson, Abigail Larson, Jody Kubitz, Zachary Kubitz, Matthew Kubitz, Verna (Hagen) & Bruce Leitch, Daniel Bruce Leitch, John Leitch, Amanda Leitch, Kathleen Leitch Gibson, Michael Gibson, Thomas Gibson, Elizabeth Gibson, Mary Ann (Hagen) Leitch, Liz Leitch Sell, Samantha Sell, David Sell, Steve Leitch, Brad Leitch, Brittany Leitch, Gayle Leitch Kelly, McKenzie Kelly, Nick Kelly, Laurie Leitch, Helen L. (Bjergo) Gookin, Elizabeth Gookin Belcourt, Anne Elizabeth Belcourt, Rena Belcourt, Kathleen Gookin Ford, Emilia Ford, Mary Gookin Comstock, Vincent Comstock, Joyce Niemi, Jane Handerhan, Miranda Handerhan, Kayla Arbuckle, Claire Kippola, Steven Kippola, Paul Niemi, Christopher Niemi, Glen Logas, Michelle Logas, Joslyn Anderson, Perry Anderson, Timothy Anderson, Jesse Anderson, Susan Ackerman, Kendra Ackerman, Sandra Van Dyke, Bradly Van Dyke, Kyle Van Dyke, Keleigh Van Dyke, Stacy Boese, Amber Boese, Marlene Kugler, Debra Messer, Craig Messer, Tamela Collins, Jonathan Collins, Luke Collins, Celine Collins, Kim Dewey, Barton Dewey, Darcie Combs, Ali Drechsel, Carly Dewey, Scott Kugler, Shannon Leine, Abigail Leine, Orrie Leine, Seth Leine, Jessica Schroeder, Madeline Schroeder, Brandon Schroeder, Grace Schroeder, Danielle Wegner, Jordon Wegner, Tyler Wegner, Madison Wegner, Lorraine A. Isaacson, Judy K. Lamphron, Paul Lamphron, Jennifer Lamphron, Diane L. Vetch, Justin Vetch, Olivia Vetch, Leah Vetch, Derek Vetch, Allen Bjergo, Karl Bjergo, Anne Bjergo Tafoya, Sunan Bjergo Laws, Scott Bjergo, Jody Bjergo Collins. *The descendants of Michael J. Fossen and Ole J. Fossen are also descendants of Jens Fossen.*

Michael J. Fossen: Kathryn Haugen Foster, Nancy Foster Wilson, Elizabeth Foster Felt, Ruth Foster Koth, Mikkel Haugen, Dr. Marilyn Christensen, Mary Davenport Thilly, Helen Thilly, Owen Thilly, Peter Thilly, Richard B. Davenport, James L. Davenport, John T. Davenport, Alexander Wickersham Davenport, Mary Beth Jochim, Jennifer McGovern, Aedan McGovern, Ruadhri McGovern, Julie Piehl, Audrey Rose Piehl, Michael C. Fossen, Brady J. Fossen, Rona (Ken) Corrigan, Douglas (Jennifer) Spain,

Living Descendants of Charter Members

Cheryl Lonsdale, Karen (Greg) Pettinato, Amanda Pettinato, Adam Pettinato, Alyssa Pettinato, Linda Montoya, Cassandra Montoya, Kristopher Montoya, Jacob Montoya, David Lonsdale, Thomas Spain, Marie (David Lyle) Maas, Barbara Peterson, Noah Peterson, Toni (Spain) Steffenson, Jeffrey Steffenson, Derek Steffenson, Carrissa Steffenson, Sonja Seim, Meagan Seim, MacKenzie Seim, Jordan Seim, Jerad Seim, Debra Meier, Thane Meier, Savanna Meier, Cory Steffenson, Virginia (Kenneth) Millett, Kristine Gordon, Charles (Susan) Spain, Kimberley Phelan, Allison Spain, Stephanie Spain, Sylvia Reilly, Jill Yanish. *All descendants of Michael J. Fossen are also descendants of Jens Fossen.*

Ole J. Fossen: Mary Benson, Scott Benson, Rachel Benson, Jacob Benson, Nathan Benson, Emma Benson, Steven Benson, Ryan Benson, Matthew Benson, Douglas Benson, Peter Benson, Laura Benson, Andrew Benson, Eric Benson, Elsa Benson, Mitchell Benson. *All descendants of Ole J. Fossen are also descendants of Jens Fossen.*

Gunder Frigaard: James O'Shea, Sherryl E. Wilcox, Becky Arnhold, Marty P. Frigaard, Ronald J. Nelson, Julie Edwards, Mark Rushfeldt, Dean Rushfeldt, Thomas Nelson, Elizabeth Roth, David Sinner, Thomas Sinner, Lori Tompkins, Brenda Kay DuPlessis, Melinda Sue Wozniak, John Todd DuPlessis, Sarah Ann Zunich, Julie Ann Zunich, Becky Lynn Zunich, Scott Edward DuPlessis, Madeline Michelle DuPlessis, Claire Ann Wozniak, Marcia Frigaard Steil, Lisa Lomas, Madison Lomas, MacKenzie Lomas, Heather Steil, Donald E. Tinguely

Otto Furreness: Orville Furreness, Beth Furreness Chell, Carly Chell, Cody Chell, Jon Furreness, Donald Kolstad, Michael Kolstad, Ione Furreness, Jasmine Chapman, Bette Kolstad Johnson, Jason Johnson, Marian Anderson Kubitz, Pamela Kubitz Bice, Nancy Kubitz Larson, Tyler Larson, Abigail Larson, Jody Kubitz, Zachary Kubitz, Matthew Kubitz

John Furuness: None found

Albert Gjerset: Kenneth W. Bateman, Mark Bateman, David B. Gjerset, Moira Bateman Beeman

Magnus Gjerset: Joan Gjerset Cushman, Richard Gjerset, Douglas Gjerset, Marlene Gjerset Teigen, Pat Kelzer Rogers, Mary Phillips, Andrea Beede, Carolynne Beede, Paul Beede, Laura Beede, Robert Teigen, April Teigen, Natalie Teigen, Kathryn Mansergh, Jacquelyn Mansergh, Douglas Gjerset, Kristin Gjerset, Taya Hurlbut, Chloe Hurlbut, Kaarin Gjerset

Oluf Gjerset: No children

O. [Ole] A. Grande: Graham Grande, Lauren Grande Scarborough, Jessica Scarborough, Nicholas Scarborough, Jessica Merritt Scarborough, Nicholas E. Scarborough, Karen Grande Vaillant, Andrew Vaillant, Karlee Vaillant, Andrew T. Vaillant, Karlee Vaillant, Donna Grande Ward, Gary Largent, David Largent, David Wee, Elizabeth Day Wee, Mary Wee Maxwell

Christian Haarsager /Christ Horsager: Birger Horsager, Ernie Horsager, Linda Harriman, Joan Sateren, Jean Horsager Miller, Neil Horsager, Sonia Kaltvedt, Avis Hovland

Elias Haarsager / Elias Jensen Horsager: Dennis Haarsager

John P. Haave: No children

John P. Haave, Jr.: John Gunderson

Edw. Haldorsen: No children

Martin O. Hall: None found

Jonas O. Hallan: None found

S. [Sivert] O. Hammer: Mrs. Erling (Hjordis) Skugrud, Mrs. Joy Toso, Stanley Toso, Conni Toso Axness, Karen Toso Froslie, Carol Toso Honeik, Amy Toso Meyer, Kayla Toso, Jessica Toso Holland, Molly Toso, Arthur Hammer, Jr., Joe Hammer, Mark Hammer, Brad Hammer, Nikki Hammer, Sami Hammer, Melissa

Living Descendants of Charter Members

Hayden, Jacob Hayden, Josie Hayden, Dalton Hayden, Christi Evenson, Jed Evenson, Chloe Evenson, Stacy Froslie Lindbom, Bethany Froslie, Kyle & Desi Froslie, Owen Froslie, Alyson Froslie, Michelle Honcik Nitschke, Isabella Nitschke, Lucas Nitschke, Jennifer Honcik, Justin Axness, Jesse & Jay Axness, Joseph & Teri Axness, Jay Axness

J. [Jacob] O. Hatling: John A. Hatling, Anne Hatling, Elizabeth Hatling, Jacob Hatling, Joseph Hatling, Maren Hatling, Noble Hatling, Amanda Hatling, Abigail Hatling, Bonnie Brown, Kathy Johnson, Paul Ziese, Grant Hatling, Avona Carroll, Andrew Hatling, Gwen Hatling Ziese, Michael Kent Hatling, William Ross Hatling, Maxwell Hatling, Hannah Hatling, Becky Lovgren, Darlene L. & Robert L. Munneke, Daryl B. Hatling, Gloria E. & John Buchan

J. [John] Hatlinghus: No children

O. [Ole] C. Hauan: Martin Hauan, Marean Hauan Anderson, Virginia R. Hauan, J. W. Hauan

Bernt B. Haugan: None found

O.B. Haugen: No children

John Hindrum: None found

John Hogstad: Descendants of his wife: Vidkunn Berg, Hilde Følstad

Arnt O. Huseby: Thomas Wayne Huseby, Todd P. Huseby, John Richard, Huseby, Nacy Caroll Huseby DeBaca, Doris Huseby Franzese, James Lawrence Huseby, Holly Huseby Loving, Heidi Elizabth Huseby Slater, Stuart Sydney, Scott Alen Huseby, Steven Stuart Huseby, Jennifer Jean Huseby, Jill Kristen Pellior, Joshua David Hamm, Syndney Bernard, Huseby, Jr., Ashley Nicole Huseby O'Dell, Jessica Lynn Huseby, Irvin Charles Huseby, Jessica Lyn Huseby

Severin (Sam) Huseby: Keith Gates, Teri Katherine Popp

Ulrick Huus: Terrelyn Huss Sweeney, Gerald D. Huss

Endre Ingebretsen (Andrew Ingebretson): Harvey Evenson, Clifford E. Evenson, Bonnie Swanson, John B. Evenson, Orrin E. Evenson

Jacob Jensen: Ivan Raymond Jensen, Rodney & Vicki Jensen, Ronald Ivan Jensen, Rodger Alan Jensen,

Paul Johanson: None found

Fred Johnsen: None found

Christian Johnson: None found

Martin Johnson: Thomas E. Hiedeman, Gerald Hiedeman, John A. Hiedeman, Jill Hiedeman Busching, Bruce Hiedeman, Bryan Hiedeman, Dennis Keith Hiedeman, Jerry L. Hiedeman, Marshall L. Hiedeman, Rhonda A. Hiedeman, Amy Hiedeman, Thomas E. Hiedeman, Keith A. Hiedeman, Kelly D. Hiedeman, John A. Hiedeman, Justin A. Hiedeman, Joshua S. Hiedeman, Shelly R. Hiedeman, John E. Hiedeman, Sheila A. Hiedeman, Melissa J. Hiedeman, Bruce J. Hiedeman, Anthony D. Reff, Apryl J. Reff, Andrea J. Reff, Jill M. Hiedeman, Jeremy S. Busching, Joel W. Busching, Bruce L. Hiedeman, Bryan M. Hiedeman, Eric M. Hiedeman, Toni M. Hiedeman, Shawn L. Hiedeman, Amanda R. Hiedeman, Erica J. Hiedeman, Marcy Ugstad, Sandy Walker, Kay Johnson Hoopes, Carleton A. Sperati, Charles R. Sperati, Christine L. Sperati, Christopher J. Sperati, William E. Sperati, Jacob E. Sperati, Joshua E. Sperati, Rebecca M. Sperati, Solveig Sperati Korte, Kendra M. Korte, Kirsten L. Korte, Beverly Sperati Arneson, Georgianne E. Arneson, Beverly Sperati Weeks, Charles P. Sperati, Susan M. Sperati, Albert M. Johnson, Mark D. Johnson, Martin Johnson, Sonja Lorraine Johnson, Dustin Johnson, Tasha Johnson, Quinten A. Johnson, Paula Johnson Thomas, Roy R. Thomas, Janelle M. Thomas, Michael "Eric" Johnson, Lucy Johnson Nelson, Donald L. Nelson, Rebecca E. Nelson, Benjamin D. Nelson, Dale E. Nelson, Anne V. Nelson, Byron D. Nelson, Peter L. Nelson, Lindsay A. Nelson, David A.

LIVING DESCENDANTS OF CHARTER MEMBERS

Nelson, Joanna K. Nelson, Jessica L. Nelson, Jacob D. Nelson, Louise Johnson Snyder, Fremont J. Snyder, Paige Snyder Lord, Sandra Snyder Yager, Duane A. Yager, Janis T. Wiser, Jason S. Johnson, Curtis A. Snyder, Tobi Lynn Snyder, Curtis A. Snyder, Jr., Kim Snyder Jenkins, Melonie Jenkins, Japhy T. Jenkins, Armand F. Johnson, Karen Johnson Iverson, Scott Iverson, Sherry Iverson Fullerton, Dennis Johnson, Scott D. Johnson, Bree Denise Johnson, Dennis Johnson, Lester Johnson, Trisia Johnson, Debbie Sue Johnson, Janelle Johnson, Dale Johnson, Philip A. Johnson, Owen M. Johnson, Annelise Johnson, Ryan Johnson, Danny Johnson, Larry S. Johnson, James Johnson, Kay L. Johnson, Marshall D. Hooper, Asia L. Hooper, Tammy K. Johnson

Theo Johnson: Rebecca Kuehnel, Christopher M. Kuehnel, Peter N. Kuehnel, David A. Kuehnel, Thomas L. Kuehnel, Samio P. Kuehnel, Maria K. Kuehnel, Natasha C. Kuehnel, Jean M. Kuehnel, Victoria L. Kuehnel, Fernando R. Kuehnel, Fernando R. Kuehnel II, John A. Kuehnel, HoChang C. Kuehnel, Adriano P. Kuehnel, Austin P. Kuehnel, Caleb R. Kuehnel, Dakota D. Kuehnel, Roberto N. Kuehnel, Tyrone A. Kuehnel, Tyler F. Kuehnel, Steven M. Kuehnel, Ellesandra R. Kuehnel, Nicholas A. Kuehnel, Meghan R. Kuehnel, LTCOL Ret. Conrad L. Johnson, Tony Lee Johnson, Conrad Johnson, Lezlie Johnson Thompson, Ashley Johnson, Daunte Smith, Linda Lee Johnson Uhl, Lisa Ann (Johnson) Scherbenske, Julia Scherbenske, Lindsey Scherbenske, Cole Scherbenske, Jonathan Scherbenske, Amanda Celina Uhl, Aaron Jeffrey Uhl, Deborah J. Geske, Dr. F. Jon Geske, Jane Huerta, Benjamin Geske, Erec Toso, Kyle Schrag-Toso, Sean Schrag-Toso, Kathryn (Pederson) Knutson, KC Toso, John Toso, Andrew Toso, Gustav Andrew Toso, Norman Toso, Lisa Moreland, Sarah Geuder, Margaret Leake, Doris (Pederson) Enderson, Carrie Enderson Thompson, Benjamin M. Thompson, Rebekah Thompson Ohren, Mark Ohren, Mary Enderson Link, Landon Link, Aaron Link, Mary Link, Gerrald T. Enderson, Emily Enderson, Liza Enderson, Kati Enderson, Bethany Enderson, Laura Enderson, Joel D. Enderson, Stethany

Enderson, Charles E. Pederson, Loiland Pederson, Brandon C. Pederson, Richard Pederson, Barbara (Bergeson) Olson, James Bergeson, Steven Bergeson, JoEllen (Bergeson) De Cesear, Margaret Pederson-Martin, Mary Pederson-Martin, Grace Pederson-Martin, Eric Pederson-Martin, Lily Pederson-Martin

Anton & Caroline Jordahl: Doris Berger Couch, Eugene Couch, Carol J. Couch, Lori L. Couch, Clinton W. Couch, Wanda Couch Chilton, Tevin F. Chilton, Kimberly Chilton Squires, Alexa Squires, Donald E. Berger, Oscar "Buster" Berger, Kenny Berger, Suzie Berger, Danny Berger, Ashley Holland, James E. Holland, Kyle Holland, Karen Holland Davis, Mayson Davis, Jocelyn Berger, Tammera Berger Jones, Britney A. Jones, Chad E. Jones, Chelsi Jones, Terry D. Berger, Timothy D. Berger, Irene Berger Correa, Diane Correa Kemp, Rita Correa Liberto, Shawna Liberto Taylor, Megan Liberto, Linda Correa Baker, Lyda (Berger) Holland, Audry Couch Conner, Jack E. Conner, Jack Conner, Austin D. Conner, Robert W. Conner, Abigail D. Conner, Cheryl Conner Stout, Jacqueline Stout, Troy Stout, David M. Correa, Amiee Correa, Sara Correa, Nichole Correa, Bobbie Correa

Johan Knudsen: None found

Eilert Koefod: Dana Koefod, Debbie & Tom Healy, Jeff Healy

Peter & Mariane Lein: Eric Lein, Kristin Lein, R. Kurt Lein, Alisa Lein, Beldonna Brown

O. [Ole] O. Lerfald: Mike Miller, David & Linda Lerfald, Charles Lerfald, Mary Lerfald Shillinglaw, Ashley Shillinglaw, Jonathan Shillinglaw, Frank Lerfald, Dennis Lerfald, Beverly Lerfald Molter, Sharon Mooty, Dianne Billmyre, Sandra Kvern, Ted Miller, Wendy Weigel

S. [Sivert] O. Leirfallom: Frida Leirfallom Layton, Jarl S. Leirfallom, Leif Leirfallom, Linda Leirfallom Brewer, Lisa Leirfallom Doyscher, Kristofer Leirfallom, Ms. Signe Leirfallom, Diana Nelson, Eugene S. Layton

Living Descendants of Charter Members

Jon Lervik: John C. Lervick

Peter A. Loktu: Matthew J. Drechsel

Mrs. Odin Løseth [Astrid Ekker]: William James Loseth, Helene Loseth Krause, Susan Loseth Mickelson, Mary Loseth Andersen, John F. Loseth

Edvard Lund: A niece, Marjorie Lund Sorenson

J. [John] Lyng: Maureen Torgusson, Darren Torgusson, Mishon Torgusson, Tiffany Torgusson

Emil Middelfart: None found

Stasius Norgaard/Nordgaard: John & Char Nordgaard, Jeanette Nelson, Cynthia Kay Luna, Kathy Lynn Denooyer, Dawn Martin, Tyler Martin, Bailey Martin, Heather Martin, Jeremy Martin, Cami Ferguson, Donald Toso, Stanley (Deb) Toso, Conni Toso Axness, Karen Toso Froslie, Carol Toso Honeik, Amy Toso Meyer, Kayla Toso, Jessica Toso Holland, Molly Toso, Stacy Froslie Lindbom, Kyle Froslie, Alyson Froslie, Bethany Froslie, Michelle Honcik Nitschke, Jennifer Honcik, Justin Axness, Jesse & Jay Axness, Joseph & Teri Axness, Isabella & Lucas Nitschke, Owen Froslie, Elli Meyer, Ordean Haarstad, Joyce Haarstad Boese, Dale A. Boese, Jeffery Boese, Jerome & Joy Toso, Norman Toso, Timothy Toso, Mary Ann Anderson, Carol Nordgaard, Jeanette Nelson, Daniel Nelson, Ezekiel Nelson, Zachariah Nelson, Malachi Nelson, Micah Nelson, David Nelson, Lynette Heinzen, Alexander Heinzen, Christina Heinzen, Zachary Heinzen, Doyle H. Boese, Daryl S. Boese, Michael Boese, Steven Boese, Marc Boese, Joshua Boese, Hannah Boese, Darla Boese Gorghuber, Sarah Gorghuber, Robert Gorghuber, Daniel Gorghuber, Stephanie Gorghuber, Haleigh Boese, Ronald Erickson, Nancy Weik, Larry Norgaard, Gary Norgaard

Ole Nygaard: Steven Gilbertson, Vernon Gilbertson, Alice Ness, Helene N. Pavlowich

Mads Olson & Gjertru Pedersdatter: Tim Schnitzer, Robert D. Schnitzer, Virginia Mae Olson Root, Russell T. Schnitzer, Pamela J. Schnitzer, Gabriel M. Noah, Adam T. Noah, Ashley R. Noah, Sharon (Root) Christensen, Wendy Kay Christensen, David Allan Christensen, Annika Christensen, Kyra Christensen, Thomas W. Woody, Dave & Kathy Rootham, Jan Rootham, Jamie L. Rootham, Diana M. Rootham, Lori Olson Koenig, Darrell Olson, Donald Brahmer, Patricia Moore McGinnis, George C. Landrith III, Peter Jordan Landrith, David King Landrith, Mary Landrith, Rebecca Landrith, Gerald D. Nelson, Richard L. Nelson, Jean Nelson, Linda Nelson, Debbie Nelson, Terri Nelson, Marchita Olson, Darrell D. Olson, Laurel J. Olson, Bruce A. Olson, Kathleen S. Olson, Perry N. Olson, Peter J. Olson, Faith N. Olson, Mark A. Olson, Polly Ann Olson, Paige Jean Olson

Olaus Olson: Carol McFarland, Ron Olson

Oluf E. Orstad: Mary Nold, Michael Nold

Lars O. Overmoen (Lars Olsen): Arlen B. Brunsvold

Christ Pederson: Beverly Koval, Carla S. Koval, Nordahl Flaten Jr.

Nils Pederson: None found

Erik Peterson: Kenneth & Mary Nash, Paul M. Nash, Donald B. Nash, Brock Nash, Keith M. Nash, Kyle Nash, Kara Jo Nash, Karsten Nash, Marjorie Jacobson, Andrew Jacobson, Grant Jacobson, Abigail Jacobson, Marlow K. Nash, Melody Nash, Sofia Nash, Haakon Georg Nash, Kermit J. Nash, Bruce & Brady Nash, Kenny Nash, Jennifer Nash Maltby, Benjamin Nash, Noah Nash, Karen Brewer, Bill Brewer, Beverly & Mike Gebhart, Gregg Gebhart, Andrew Gebhart, Megan Gebhart, Michelle Burgard, Jeff Gebhart, Daniel Gebhart, Brandon Gebhart, Scott Gebhart, Chase Gebhart, Casey Gebhart, Haley Gebhart, Rose Gebhart, Cristina Gebhart, Jennifer Argue, Hannah Argue, John Argue, Michael Argue, Joseph Argue, Matthew Burgard, Jill Joyce, Joran Joyce, Benjamin Joyce, Michael Burgard, Zachary Gebhart, Ernest & Jean Nash, Brad Nash, Audrey Nash, Jacob Nash, Jared Nash,

Living Descendants of Charter Members

Perry Nash, Preston Nash, Courtney Nash, Wanita Sletten, Joel Nash, Stephen Nash, Nathaniel Nash, Christine Nash, Philip Nash, Naomi Johnson, Lucas Johnson, Emily Johnson, Sonia Muller, Anthony Thompson, Brittany Thompson, Mathew & Marc Johnson, Erin Fontaine, Nicole Johnson, Ashton Johnson, Jason Kamphaugh, Hannah Kamphaugh, Isaac Kamphaugh, Peter Kamphaugh, Joshua Kamphaugh, Chelsa Nash, Beatrice Nash Faust, Nathan Faust, Marco Faust, Timothy Faust, Monica Faust Cox, Benjamin Cox, Jeremiah Cox, Jonathan Faust, Clinton Faust, Eric Faust, Gregory Faust, Rachel Faust, Jared Faust, Tyler Faust, Zachary Faust, Ethan Faust, Mitchell Faust

Cornelius Petterson: Patricia Peterson Jouppi, Betty L. Rovang, Eric W. Rovang, Kirk E. Rovang, Rolf A. Rovang, Kirsten Rovang Olson, Peter J. Rovang, Gerald Peterson, Bob Peterson, David Peterson, Carol Peterson Donaldson, Krista L. Peterson Olia, Mark E. Peterson, Glen R. Peterson, Marion Dyrud Peterson, Jean Marie Neumann, Lisa Ann Neumann, Paul Robert Neumann, Gerald Peterson

Ingolf Petterson: None

Martin Rathe: Pastor Mark Rathe

Ditlef B. Ristad: Rev. Robert N. Ristad, Jr., Edwin Ristad, Karin Ristad Puchner, Mary Carbon, Edwin S. Ristad

B. [Brynjulf] Rønning: None found

(Bernt) Martin Rosvold: Moris Hoversten, Helen Hoversten Mikelson, Philip Hoversten, Tiffany Hoversten, Schuyler Hoversten, Whitney Hoversten, Barbara Hoversten, Nancy Battey, Anne R. Battey, Lindsay C. Battey, Peter Hoversten, Larry D. Mikelson, Danyel Mikelson, Mathew S. Mikelson, Kathy Mikelson Olsen, Karen Roth, Kay Mikelson Wick, Wendy K. Wick, Brandon D. Wick, Thelma Hoversten Simmons, Joan Simmons Wenzel, Todd Wenzel, Kristin Wenzel, Stacy Wenzel, Jennifer Wenzel, Judy Simmons Frost, Gary Simmons, Rev. Henry & Janice Hoversten, Bill Hoversten, Dan Hoversten, Sydney A. Hoversten,

Daniel Hoversten II, Paul Hoversten, Adam Hoversten, Carol Pepper, Ariel Pepper, Arvid Hoversten, Ruth Thompson, Claire E. Dorton, Clyde Thompson, Timothy Thompson, Patrick Thompson, Kenneth Rosvold, Earl Winston Schulz, Eric Evan Schulz, Karl David Schulz, Irene Hausken, Teresa A. Sharkey, Brianna Sharkey, Erin Sharkey, Gregory O. Hausken, Toril Hausken, Ryley Hausken, Keely Hausken, Kian Hausken, Jeffrey D. Hausken, Thomas C. Hausken, Zachary E. Hausken, Griff Hausken, Guthrie Hausken, Minerva Thompson, Doris Nagel, Gail Nagel Erickson, Lori Scott, Mary Hauck, Tad C. Hauck, Jason Hauck, Sarah Hauck, Elizabeth M. Fulton, Emma Fulton, Maria Fulton, Robert D. Hauck, Katherine Peterson, David A. Peterson, Brittanie Peterson, Brooke Peterson, Karen K. Dahmer, Stephan Dahmer, Kirsten Dahmer, Ali Dahmer, Lisa L. Climo, Ayrton Climo, Ruth Hutchins, Gretchen L. Shermann, Taylor Shermann, Nicholas Shermann, Bridget D. Harter, Jennifer Harter, Todd L. Crosby, Rachel Crosby, Hannah Crosby, Mark Crosby, Beth C. Macaulay, Nichole Foster, Stephanie Foster, Brice Foster, Grace Macaulay, Laurin Hoversten

Jon Røst (Johan Sve): James Rost, Clinton Rost

Mrs. O. A. Rustad: Richard E. Rustad, Robert Rustad, Katherine Estrem Rustad, Daryl B. Hatling, Darlene L. & Robert L. Munneke, Gloria E. & John Buchan

Johannes P. Schei: Lujean Kugler, Roxanne & Scott Lofgren, Amanda Jo Lofgren, Jessica Lynn Lofgren, Norna J. & Harvey L. Delong, Nancy & Earl Seeba, Arnold Seeba, Alvin Seeba, Amy Seeba, Carla Seeba, Vicki & Gary Jeppesen, Bradley Jeppesen, Charles Jeppesen, Elizabeth Jeppesen, Ryan Jeppesen, Geraldine C. Berg, Dean Berg, Jennifer Berg, Kari Berg, Steven Berg, Taylor Berg, Connor Berg, MarDee Berg, Ashley Miller, Matthew Miller, LiAnn M. Rising, David M. Rising, Frankie Carroll, Tiffany C. Carroll, Jeremy Carroll Patton, Julie Carroll, Janette Anderson Porter

Living Descendants of charter members

Ole J. Schei: Mark William Wilke, Rachel Wilke, Kristin A. McTeague, Bill & Paula Wilke, Peter Jay Wilke, Jennifer Wilke Willens, Dillon Wilke, Ann Margaret Wilke, Meredith W. Kenyon, Charles Kenyon, Lauren Kenyon, John C. Wilke

Haakon Selness/Salness: Linda Haukedahl, Duane Salness

Theo [Theodore O.] Sjørdal: Margaret R. Miller, Laura & Greg Halldin, Julian Sjordal, Jeanette Torp, Steven Torp, Melissa Torp, Brad Torp, Noel Cadwell, Sanford Cadwell, Harriett Kern, Virgil Polland, Sara Buehler, Dennis Pollard, Theodore Pollard, Jeff Halldin, Andrew Halldin

Iver O. Skistad: Gaylen & Shelley Skistad, Robert Skistad, Charles & Laurice Harstad Swenson

S. [Sigurd] M. & Oline (Dahl) Skrove: Sidney Skrove, Wyonne Adamsen, Norma McCoy, Viola Behrends, Leona Zimmerman

O. S. Sneve: None found

Olaf A. Solberg: Gary F. Goodwin

A. [Anfinn] Solem: None found

C.P. Stav: Mark Asleson, Margaret Asleson Holte, Richard Asleson, David Holte, Eldon K. Rund, David H. Rund, Rodney A. Pletan, Lynnae L. Pletan, Sheila S. Pletan, Gina M. Pletan, David O. Miller, Robert Asleson. Kathryn Asleson, Sharon Odegard, Keith Odegard, Neil Odegard, Lyle E. Skinnemoen, Warren A. Skinnemoen, Robert L. Pletan, Cynthia D. Pletan, Paul K. Rund, Diane C. Rund, Sidney K. Pletan, Carol N. Pletan, Beth J. Pletan, Blaine L. Pletan, Brian A. Pletan, Ernest M. Pletan, Ernest M. Pletan, Jr., Judy A. Pletan, Linda J. Pletan, Richard W. Pletan, Gerald W. Pletan, Gary R. Pletan, Trudy M. Pletan, Dale A. Pletan, Kevin R. Pletan, Dwight G. Pletan, Phyllis Pletan Nelson, Larry J. Nelson, Dean W. Nelson, La Vonne J. Nelson, Joyce M. Pletan Peterson, Ward D. Peterson, Loren R. Peterson, Jane N. Peterson, Kristine J. Peterson, Donna J. Peterson, Marlys

E. Pletan, Carol E. Vaagen, Loris O. Vaagen, Loretta O. Vaagen, Miles D. Vaagen, Peggy Vaagen, Paula A. Vaagen, Gerald M. Vaagen, Ralph E. Pletan, Dale R. Pletan, Elaine R. Pletan, Audrey B. Pletan, Bruce J. Pletan, Clifford J. Pletan, Melissa Pletan, Heather Pletan, Donald L. Pletan, Ronald L. Pletan, Bonita S. Pletan, Warren R. Pletan, Laure Jean Pletan, Rocky D. Pletan, Steven J. Pletan, Elaine D. Pletan, Loretta Pletan Hoversten, Timothy L. Hoversten, Gloria Ann Hoverstein, Michael D. Pletan, Jill M. Pletan, Amy Ann Pletan, Lorraine Vranna, Warren Vranna, James Monson, Karen Monson, Brian Monson, Kathryn Monson, Brad Monson, Robert Pletan, Merlin Pletan, Orion L. Pletan, Julie Pletan, Pam Pletan, Michael J. Pletan, Mary Ann Pletan, Raymond C. Pletan, Chance Pletan, Brandy Lynn Pletan, Zachary Pletan, Christa G. Pletan, Dustin R. Pletan, Cecilia M. Pletan, Julia E. Pletan, Gabriel L. Pletan, Ezekiel J. Pletan, Jeremiah H. Pletan, Jacob A. Pletan, Noreen L. Pletan, Paul Halderson, Roger A. Pletan, Candice L. Pletan, Richard L. Asleson, Wesley Asleson, Daniel Asleson, Cynthia L. Asleson, Wendy C. Erickson, Randal G. Erickson, Rebecca C. Erickson, Diahann M. Holte, Mark O. Asleson, Robert B. Asleson, Andrew W. Asleson, Keri L. Skinnemoen, Teresa S. Skinnemoen, Joan E. Pletan, Michael E. Pletan, Anne C. Pletan, Melissa Ann Nelson, Darryl P. Nelson, Laralynn D. Nelson, Peter J. Nelson, Andrew P. Nelson, Natalie J. Rund, Angela M. Rund, Eric D. Rund, Heidi Jo Rund, Paula K. Rund, Jason K. Rund, Meghan L. Rund, Jena Chun Boen, Dillon E. Boen, Daniel S. Pletan, Bonnie L. Pletan, Carmen K. Pletan, Lila Marie Pletan, Shawn K. Pletan, Sheila Kae Pletan, Dean Gordon Hauge, Todd J. Zenda, Shawn L. Pletan, Craig A. Pletan, Crystal R. Pletan, Monica Janssen, Rebecca Janssen, James Janssen, David M. Irish, Brian J. Irish, Gail D. Irish, Jerilee Pletan, Wendy Pletan, Royal Woodward, Chad G. Pletan, Casey A. Pletan, Cody A. Pletan, Kristie Lynn Pletan, Lisa Marie Pletan, Steven Pletan, Ryan J. Pletan, Robyn R. Pletan, Rita Joy Pletan, Kandra D. Nelson, Cole A. Nelson, Thane P. Nelson, Lee B. Peterson, Lauren E. Peterson, Robbie Howell, Arif Ali, Nissa Ali, Nathan Ali, Sara Saleem, Harris P. Saleem, Adam Saleem, Hannah Saleem, Zane D. Schaefer, Emily

Living Descendants of Charter Members

K. Schaefer, Curtis R. Schaefer, Augustus Detrick, Tilia Detrick, Linea Detrick, Shawn E. Gjermundson, Brett Gjermundson, Audrey K. Marcusen, Dane C. Marcusen, Ray W. Bluemer, Jr., Barton L. Bluemer, Kaleena Bluemer, Ellen Marie Vaagen, Laura Pletan, Garaint Pickering, Ryianydd Pickering, Elizabeth Pletan, Phillip J. Pletan, Erica Pletan, Brandi Kennedy, Justin Kennedy, Cory D. Pletan, Kyle C. Pletan, Thomas Pletan, Joseph Monson, Kristi Monson, Reed Monson, Nancy Stephens, Vyonne Stephens, Byron Stephens, Rachel Stephens, Luke Stephens, Nathanel Stephens, Lydia B. Stephens, Peder Randal Erickson, Elizabeth A. Erickson, David Erickson, Abigail M. Erickson, Madeline C. Lacey, Kate E. Lacey, Justin P. Wilson, Gabriella N. Wilson, Axel V. Nierste, Erica L. Rau, Melissa M. Rau, Kevin W. Rau, Ryan T. Pagois, Ellen A. Pagois, Clara A. Pagois, Marie C. Schield, Emily J. Schield, Noah W. Yager, Elisabeth G. Yager, Sydney J. Pletan, Samuel Jens Pletan, Anna M. Nelson, Joshua P. Nelson, Benjamin I. Nelson, Lucas T. Nelson, Zachary J. Nelson, Ashley N. Seibert, Emma Lou Rund, Jonathan S. Pletan, Joshua W. Pletan, Micah T. Munion, Andrew T. Munion, Noah W. Munion, Savanah L. Koestler, Johan J. Koestler, Joseph J. Koestler, Cassie D. Koestler., Jessica L. Stepardson, Joshua D. Stepardson, Shelby-Shaun Retherford, Preston J. Retherford, Jaydon B. Zenda, Jenna Leigh

B. [Bernt] M. Stene: No children

Isak Strinden: Duane Strinden, Tina Marie Strinden Miller, Christopher N. Strinden, Eric N. Strinden, Thomas D. Ahlin, Lillian Jeanette Nelson, Marcelle Strinden, Dean R. Strinden, Constance Fjestad Michealson, Harlon E. Strinden, Jenny & Steve Griep, Ruth Johnson, Dale Michaelson, Charles Michaelson, Tristan Michaelson, Constance Miller, Lori Herman, Cassandra Herman, Rachel Herman, Matthew Vivirito, Miles Vivirito, Sedona Vivirito, Astoria Vivirito, David Tostenson, Eric Tostenson, Chad Tostenson, Donald Tostenson, Dawn Tostenson, Kasey Tostenson, Richard Fjestad, Rochelle Byklum, Matia Byklum, Lisa Ouren, Brady Ouren, Jake Ouren, Mrs.

Grace T. Strinden, Jerry & Veronica Strinden, Rory Strinden, Stephen Strinden, James & Lupe Strinden, Kristina Strinden, Reena Strinden, Rev. Eugene & Lillian Strinden, Jade Yim, Timothy Strinden, Cyndi D. Vehrencamp, Earl & Jan Strinden, Patti Prince, Natasha Prince, Caleb Prince, Deann Prince, Paul Strinden, Kyle Strinden, Kevin Strinden, Lorraine E. Berger, Edna Revland, Dorothy Osterdahl Berger, John A. & Karen Berger, Kara Berger, Ryan Berger, Andrea Berger, Michael E. Berger, Katelyn Kiester, Joshua Ian Berger, Ian Berger, Tryg Berger, Mary Lynn Firestone, Robin Osterdahl Berger, Lewis Berger, Adam Strinden, Phyllis Johnson Bachman, Nancy Johnson Bywater, Dirk M. Johnson, Jeffrey Johnson, Connor Johnson, Gabriel Johnson, William Johnson, Bruce & Sarah Halverson, Ruth Orstad, Kyle Halvorson, Susan & Michael Van Erdewyk, Christian Halverson, Steve & Heidi Case, Carol & Dennis Kost, Helen Jean & Dennis Friestad, Bertha (Trygve) Berger, Nathan Berger, Virginia Olson & Dexter Washburn, James Olson, Ruth Ann Berger Miska, Claudia Revland Siegel, Catherine Revland, Steve & Mary Revland, Paul Revland, Marcia Spenser, Eric & Teresa Halvorson, Tony & Karen Grindberg, Thomas Beadle, Ashlyn Grindberg, Chase Grindberg, Nathaniel Hall, Carol Hineman, Joel Hineman, Bridget Hineman, Jared Hineman, Susan Hall, Kirsten Juhl, Bruce Strinden, Thomas I. Strinden, Jacob Strinden, Joseph Strinden, Benjamin Strinden, Sarah Strinden, Jon E. Strinden, Andrew Strinden, Daniel Strinden, Emily Strinden, Bennet Hall, Maren Hall, Elizabeth Kudoun, Isaac Kudoun, Katie Kudoun, Kathy Rugroden, William Strinden, Theron Strinden, Alfred O. Strinden, David Strinden, Steven Strinden, Marie Strinden, Michael Strinden, Matthew Strinden, Loren Strinden, Kellen Strinden, Peter R. Strinden, Brock Strinden, Chase Strinden, Erica Strinden, Ronda & Dave Zupi, Beth Ann Zupi, L. Michael Zupi, Scott & Karen Kost, Laura Kost, Janna Kost, Sarah & Kaleif Rongstad, Bethany & Spencer Cooney, Ella Louise Cooney, Kent & Shelly Kost, Ryan Kost, Elexa Kost, Mitchell Kost, Gabe Cartes, Leo Cartes, Timothy & Staci Kost, Jacob Kost, Abbey Kost, Luke Kost, Marna

Ramnath, Maia Ramnath, Monika Ramnath, Robert T. Dahl, William L. Dahl, Richard Dahl, James O. Dahl

Anton Sumstad: Wilma Raber, ViAnne Welch, Bethany Rosa, Rachel Rosa, Vincent Rosa, Ella Eloise Hamilton, Susan Raber, Donna Erickson, Robert R. Hall, Karen S. Hall, Daniel R. Hall, Joan Hoff Johnson, Eric J. Jenson, Shawna Jenson, Blake Jenson, Mandy J. Jenson, Garret Heidinger-Jenson, Caleb Braaten, Marissa Braaten, Brett Jenson, Bishop Jenson, Benjamin Jenson, RuthAnn Johnson, Michael E. Johnson, Chelsey Johnson, Jacqueline Johnson, Kimberly Hotvedt, Kyle Hotvedt, Carole E. Johnson, Joshua Williams, Jessica Williams, Daniel F. Johnson, Jacob Johnson, Justin Johnson, Jared Johnson, Gary L. Johnson, Andrea Johnson

Thorolf Svensgaard: No children. Nephew Warren P. Svendsgaard

N. O. Svorkmo: Unknown

A. [Anton] B. Thompson: Kathryn LeBrasseur, Paul LeBrasseur, James LeBrasseur, Tara LeBrasseur, Kate LeBrasseur, Eric LeBrasseur, Owen Thompson, Harriet Stevenson, Marisa Stevenson, Kathleen Stevenson Sheehy, Barbara Stevenson, Judy Backhaus, Stirling Tomlin, Shirley Tomlin, Mary Nohre, Ann Kasper, Janice & Richard Ellingson, Jorgen Ellingson, Kristin Panowicz, Emma Panowicz, Marcia Greer, Kristin Wolfram, Joan Torgerson, Addy Thompson

John Thompson: None found

John B. Thompson: No children

Nels B. Thompson: Kenneth Roger Thompson, Mikkel R. Thompson, Victoria M. Thompson, Jay L. Thompson, Valerie F. Persson, Alexander Griffin, Tiffany Griffin, Astred Griffin, Bethe Cowan Holo, Becky Cowan, Dorothy Thompson Moody, Neal Milo Thompson, Olaf Draxten, Gerald Thompson, Elaine Thompson Burseth, Janet Jacobson, Minerva Thompson, Doris Nagel, Gail Nagel Erickson, Lori Scott, Todd L. Crosby, Mark

Crosby, Beth C. Macaulay, Helen Hoverston Mikelson, Larry D. Mikelson, Kathryn Mikelson Olsen, Angela Kay Martin, David P. Martin, Karen Mikelson Roth, Robin Roth, Katherine Roth, Michael Roth, William Roth, Kay Wick, Thelma Hoverston Simmons, Joan Simmons Wenzel, Judy Simmons Frost, Gary Simmons, Gary Palmer & Michele Burseth, Daniel Peter & Christine Burseth, Pamela E. Kucera

Benjamin Trøen: Benjamin B. Troen, David G. Troen, Ruth Gremmels, Hannah Erickson, Luther Troen, John Moe, Michael Troen

Mrs. A.A. Trovaten: Ben Trovaten

Dr. [Jorgen G.] Vigen: None found

Pastor J. [Johan] O. Wangberg: Helen L. Paul, Al & Joayne Judson

Iver M. Wick: Delores Sinclair, Louise Hexum, Douglas W. Hagen, Cheryl Godwin, Barry Hexum, Danny Hexum, Vicki Noelle,

Ove Wick: None found

T. C. Wigen: No children

Gunder Winkjer: Dean Winkjer, Kirsten Winkjer Eppinger, DeAnn Winkjer Allen, Andrea Winkjer Collin, Jonathan S. Winkjer, Virginia Halsan Deatley Brown, Russell Brown, Laura Brown Jeffery

Johannes B. Wist: Grover Wist Trytten, Joseph Perry Trytten, Joseph P. Trytten, Jr., Steven E. Trytten, Joseph S. Trytten, Tawnia L. Trytten, Hilary L. Trytten, Joseph S. Trytten, Emily Wist Trytten, Anne Trytten Keisling, Nathaniel J. Keisling, Kenneth T. Keisling, John Wist Canario, Lynne Trytten Owens, Patrick Owens, Benjamin Owens, Sean C. Owens, Julia K. Joslyn, Kaaren S. Joslyn, John M. Trytten, Jr., Holly E. Trytten, John A. Joslyn, Christine R. Joslyn, Julia K. Joslyn, Deborah A. Trytten, Melissa Trytten Zakhary

LIVING DESCENDANTS OF CHARTER MEMBERS

Einar Wold: Clayton Syvertsen

Casper T. Wollan: Graham Grande, Ann J. Settles, Dave and Sandra Teigen, Homer Rovelstad, Susan Rovelstad James

Michal A. Wollan: Michelle Cox, Dave Cox, Michael L. Wollan

T.C. Wollan: Richard D. Pihlstrom, Marlys Pihlstrom Scribner, David R. Scribner, Richard T. Pihlstrom, Richard Lee Pihlstrom, Mark Pihlstrom, Ann Pihlstrom, Maxwell L. Pihlstrom, Ava Pihlstrom, Vivian Pihlstrom, Judith Eiken Farley, Michael L. Wollan, Matthew T. Wollan, Carolyn Ann Wollan, Judy K. Wollan, Andrew J. Witthuhn, Grace K. Witthuhn, John J. Wollan, Eric. E. Wollan, Kristina C. Wollan, Thomas C. Wollan, Kathryn M. Wollan Aagard, Magdeline C. Aagard, Rachel Aagard Matteson, Martha R. Aagard, Dean R. Matteson, Peter T. Wollan, Caroline Wollan Bergman, Anna K. Wollan, Sophie E. Wollan, Ty Bergman, Henry Bergman, Harrison Bergman, Brandon Scribner, Haley Scribner, Evert Polzin, Liv Polzin, Karen Scribner Polzin, Michael L. Wollan, Matthew T. Wollan, Carolyn A. Wollan, Gregory Wollan, James Wollan, Emily Wollan, Joseph Wollan

Mange Takk!

Thanks to all our Trønderlag members and visitors who joined us at the Centennial. Thanks to the Centennial Committee members and Charter Member researchers. Thanks to the Centennial Fund contributors. Thanks to the descendants who were willing to share information and photos. Thanks to Carrol Juven for arranging entertainment from Norway. Thanks to Brekke Travel for providing luggage tags. Thanks to the Tre Lag Stevne Steering Committee for being flexible with the stevne schedule.

Special thanks to Elaine Hasleton who took on the momentous task as Centennial Chair & put many hours and much effort into the preparations for the event.

Many people contributed to the planning, development and arrangements for this Centennial Celebration. Many, many thanks to you all for your time and efforts for Trønderlag!

Best regards,

Linda K. Schwartz
President & Editor
August 9, 2008

To purchase additional copies of this book, please contact:

Norskbok Press, PO Box 14, Cary, IL 60013
Cost: $15/book plus $4 for shipping

PUBLICATION ORDER FORM

Publications from Norskbok Press

Trønderlag Centennial 1908-2008
Written in commemoration of the 100th Anniversary of the Trønderlag of America. Includes Centennial program, organization history, short biographies of all 120 Charter Members and list of "found" Descendants. Approx. 150 pages. Available August 2008

Trønderlagets Aarbog 1910
Translated version of the first Aarbok. Includes membership list, reports from the stevne in Glenwood in 1909 and Grand Forks in 1910, original Constitution and Bylaws. Indexed. Approx. 60 pages. Available Fall 2008

Aarbok 2008 – Yearbook of the Trønderlag of America
In development ... to include history, photos from Stevne 2006 & 2007 and Centennial, detailed biographies of all 120 Charter Members along with other Trønder immigrants. Orders will be taken beginning August 2008 for delivery approx. December 2008 or January 2009.

Aarbok 2006 – Yearbook of the Trønderlag of America
Includes history, Heritage Tour photos and stories, Immigrant letters, Famous Tronders and their descendants, Trønderlag Immigrant biographies; 384 pages, in English, 155 photos. Index includes approx. 2700 entries. *Great for genealogy!*

Aarbok 2005 – Yearbook of the Trønderlag of America
Includes organization history and photos, Emigration from Trøndelag, 125 Trøndelag Immigrant biographies. 424 pages, in English, 115 photos. Index includes approx. 2800 entries. *Great for genealogy!*

Please make checks payable to **NORSKBOK PRESS** and mail to:

Norskbok Press / Orders
PO Box 14
Cary, IL 60013-0014

To pay in Norwegian kroner or to use a credit card to pay, please email indicating what book(s) you wish to order and we will email you an invoice using PayPal: publisher@norskbok.com

Item	Quantity	Price	Total
Trønderlag Centennial 1908-2008 Available August 2008* ISBN:0976891131		$15.00	
Trønderlagets Aarbog 1910 (translated) – ISBN:097689114x *Available Fall 2008*		$18.00	
Aarbok 2008 – Yearbook of the Trønderlag of America / ISBN:0976891123 *Available approx. December 2008- January 2009*		$25.00	
Aarbok 2006 – Yearbook of the Trønderlag of America / ISBN:0976891115		$25.00	
Aarbok 2005 – Yearbook of the Trønderlag of America / ISBN:0976891107		$25.00	
Shipping & Handling:			
Within the U.S.		$4.00 - one book $5.00 - two books	
To Canada - Air Mail		$10.00 - one book $17.00 - two books	
To Norway - Air Mail		$18.00 - one book $32.00 - two books	
Trønderlag Member Discount $1.00 per book			
Total Enclosed (U.S. Currency)			

PLEASE PRINT

Date _____

Name _____

Address _____

City, State, Zip _____

Country _____

Phone _____

Email _____

Trønderlag Member? *Circle:* Yes / No

* **Note**: Each registered Centennial attendee will receive one Centennial book as part of their registration fee

Form T08A -06/16/08